STRATEGIES FOR MANAGING
Stress After War
VETERAN'S WORKBOOK
AND GUIDE TO WELLNESS

JULIA M. WHEALIN, PhD • LORIE T. DECARVALHO, PhD • EDWARD M. VEGA, PhD

WILEY

John Wiley & Sons, Inc.

STRATEGIES FOR MANAGING

Stress After War

*We dedicate this manual to the men and women
who bear the weight of battle in their lives.
We cannot thank you enough for your remarkable
courage, strength, and sacrifice in serving our country.
Thank you for your services, and welcome home.*

Contents

Preface

It is not only stressful being in a war, but the experience of trying to fit back into society at home can be very challenging. Getting deployed, moving to and living in a foreign country away from your family and friends, fighting a war, and then getting redeployed back to the United States, are all extremely challenging. Each of these experiences holds its own types of stress. Knowing what to expect puts you more in control of your adjustment. Having the tools to deal with problems that arise will help make the transition easier for you.

This workbook will help you know what to expect and provide you with strategies to tackle problems in your life. We have written this treatment program with over 20 years of combined clinical experience working with veterans. After speaking to and counseling many returnees, we have identified several areas that veterans told us were their most common problems. These include: stress, depression, sleep problems, anger, relationship difficulties, and transitioning back into civilian life. We have addressed all of these problem areas in this workbook, and draw on the most effective strategies to help you overcome them.

We have written this workbook so that it is practical, easy to read, and easy to follow. We have provided exercises that you can do on your own, so that you can learn the information faster and apply it right away to your daily life. By using this workbook, you can start experiencing some relief from the stress you are feeling. In this workbook, you will find:

- Tools and strategies that you can use to pinpoint your symptoms and concerns before, during, and after using this workbook

- Practical suggestions, skills, and questions to help you work at your own pace on the unique problems that you may be experiencing

- Practical handouts, worksheets, and quizzes that you can use during, and after this program to ensure continued healing and growth

This workbook is designed for veterans who have served in Operation Iraqi Freedom or Operation Enduring Freedom. However, it will also be helpful to veterans from other war theatres, such as (but not limited to) World War II, Korean War, Vietnam War, and the Persian Gulf War. The transition from the war zone can be an ongoing, gradual process. Regardless of war era, our veterans deserve our full support and esteem as they readjust to life back home.

We want to thank you, from the bottom of our hearts, for all that you have done in service to our country. We consider it an honor and a privilege to serve you.

With gratitude and respect,

JULIA M. WHEALIN, PhD
Honolulu, Hawaii

LORIE T. DeCARVALHO, PhD
Fresno, California

EDWARD M. VEGA, PhD
Atlanta, Georgia

Acknowledgments

We would like to acknowledge the contribution of the many returning warriors with whom we have spoken over the last five years as we developed and refined this treatment guide. The openness of these veterans was a key factor in helping us understand the problems faced by those experiencing combat stress. We are grateful for their willingness to share, during clinical assessments and interventions, the challenges they faced and in most cases, overcame. We remember each of them with great warmth, appreciation, and admiration.

Introduction

▶ For you, the veteran

When coming back from war, many people can feel overwhelmed. Veterans may face problems such as unwanted memories, nightmares, anxiety, and irritation. It is common for people to resist asking for help, even when things are going badly and they do not know what else to do. However, the truth is that everyone needs help at some point in his or her life. Just as during military operations you relied on battle buddies, sometimes recovering from battle means being able to reach out to others for help, and being available to help others as well. This workbook is designed to help with information, tools, and step-by-step strategies to help you adjust to being back home.

▶ How to use this workbook

This workbook covers several major areas that are problems for many returning veterans. We designed this program to be flexible in meeting your needs wherever you are right now. You can also use this workbook on your own: however, it is designed to be used with a counselor or leader. Your counselor or leader will be using a manual that we wrote, *Clinician's Guide to Treating Stress after War: Education and Coping Interventions for Veterans.* He or she may wish for you to follow along at the same time in your workbook.

Some people learn more by listening to someone. Others learn best by seeing something written out and reading it. Still others learn more by actually doing something. Each of these types of learning is used in this workbook. Based on your own personal style of learning—and what you wish to get out of this treatment program—you and your counselor can decide the best way for you to use this workbook. Here is a brief overview of what you will be learning about in this workbook.

In Chapter 1, we give you clear ways that you can cope with stress related to being in and returning from a war. We also talk about behaviors that would not help a person to heal. We discuss common reactions to war, including anxiety and depression, and what you can do to start feeling better.

In Chapter 2, we talk about stress and how it can affect you physically and psychologically. We help you to pinpoint cues or things that can indicate to you when your stress level is rising. We teach you how to monitor your stress levels, and we provide you with a lot of different positive ways to deal with stress better.

In Chapter 3, we provide you with a number of different skills and tools you can use to start feeling better. We explain the difference between things that will result in feeling depressed and things that will help you feel more like yourself again. Practicing the skills we offer you will be one of the most important choices you can make, and will help improve your quality of life.

In Chapter 4, we discuss a very common area that many veterans have problems with—sleep. We describe the stages of sleep, based on recent research. Based on this, we discuss how certain habits we have before we go to sleep can create more sleep problems. We give you concrete ways to improve your sleep habits so that you can start getting better sleep. Many returnees have nightmares or wake up feeling terrified without remembering their dreams. If you are having this problem with your sleep, we have provided solutions for dealing with this experience.

In Chapter 5, we discuss what anger is, how it can be hurtful, what healthy anger is, and how healthy anger can be helpful to us. We give you steps to monitor your anger and deal with it in ways that can be most helpful to you and other people in your life. We also discuss one very common and helpful way to deal with situations where you have a conflict with others.

In Chapter 6, we talk about common reactions that veterans have when they come back from a war zone and try to integrate back into society. We provide you with steps to deal with the changes you are facing right now. We also talk about how you can connect with society again. We give you ways to communicate well with people, and to recognize what your triggers are so that you can react better when things goes wrong in your life. This chapter is focused on practicing ways to help your transition period go more smoothly.

In Chapter 7, we discuss how you may be feeling as you reconnect with your family and friends. Many veterans experience frustration and hurt when they return from war. This is often because important people in their life do not understand what they have been through. You may feel like your family has changed and you cannot relate to them right now. It is also common for veterans to feel like they do not relate with their friends after returning from war. We will give you ways that you can deal with this stress.

In Chapter 8, we talk about how you can begin to look at your war experience, and yourself, in a different way. We provide stories about other veterans who have survived combat experiences, and how they dealt with the stress of coming back and healing. We offer you ways that you, too, can gain strength and grow from your experiences in war.

This workbook is designed to help you heal from your war experiences. Your current retransition from the war zone is a period for the natural healing process to take place. Before battle, soldiers are provided with armor to prevent physical injuries. This workbook will provide the armor you need to be resilient to psychological injuries. You have trained in the military and so you know that there are skills that you have learned that require consistent practice. Healing also happens when you learn and practice coping tools to deal with problems. Answering the questions in this workbook honestly and openly and doing the exercises we have suggested will help you to feel better. Like anything else in life, you will get out of this what you put into it. Know that it is worth the effort!

▶ Format of the workbook

■ Section title

We wrote the clinician's guide and workbook so that they can be used together at the same time. The titles of each section in your workbook will correspond with the titles and information in your therapist's guide. This way, you can work closely together and it is easier for you to access information and focus on your healing process.

■ When to talk to your doctor

Near the end of every chapter, we list a few questions that we ask you to take a look at. Please answer the questions honestly and openly, for your benefit. If you find that you answer yes to a number of the questions, it would be a good idea to seek out help and support from a trained professional.

■ Homework/On your own

You will feel better if you practice the tools we give you in this workbook. However, like any other skill that you try to develop, improvement will come only when you frequently use these tools in your life. The more you practice them, the better you will begin to feel.

■ Quizzes

We provide you with short quizzes after each chapter so that you can test how much you have learned and what you remember. We designed these quizzes to be fairly simple, but to help jog your memory about what is important for you to recall. Please take the time to do these quizzes, either with your therapist or on your own. Doing so will help strengthen your recall of the tools we give you, and this will help you feel stronger. We have also included the answers to the quizzes in the Appendix, so that you may review your answers after you have completed them.

▶ The Clinician's Guide

In addition to this workbook, we developed a companion manual that your counselor or group leader may be using, called the *Clinician's Guide to Treating Stress After War: Education and Coping Interventions for Veterans*. We designed this set so that you can have the maximum benefit in your treatment process. If you are working with a therapist, it would be a good idea to have him or her use the *Clinician's Guide* while you go through the workbook. Working on these strategies together will be like having a coach who can maximize the skills you will learn.

▶ When to get additional help

Returnees with combat stress go through a normal transitional period that includes mild problems such as sleep problems and irritability. However, some veterans may need additional professional help for more severe problems—such as violence, suicidality, and substance abuse. This workbook intervention is not appropriate for everyone. If you are suffering from a major disorder and are not being treated for that disorder, it is important to get additional care from a qualified mental health professional.

If you are suffering from any of the following, we recommend that you receive additional care:

■ Thoughts of harming yourself

■ Thoughts of harming someone else

■ Feeling overwhelmed

■ Not being able to function (such as not being able to go to work or care for your children)

■ Having hallucinations or delusions (such as seeing or hearing things that are really not there)

■ Abusing drugs or alcohol

Additionally, if you have a coexisting severe disorder—such as psychosis—you are unlikely to benefit from this workbook until you are stabilized and followed by a mental health professional who is able to treat that disorder.

Professionals qualified to provide mental health care will usually have a doctoral-level degree (e.g., M.D., Ph.D., Psy.D.) or at least a master's degree (e.g., M.S., L.C.S.W., C.S.W., M.A.). Psychologists and other professionals with special training in posttraumatic stress disorder (PTSD) will be able to provide more advanced treatment for trauma memories, nightmares, and bereavement. See the resource section of this workbook for recommendations about where and when to get help.

Remember, if you are in a crisis, or if you are worried that you might hurt or kill yourself or someone else, you should get help immediately. Here are some hotline numbers that may be useful:

■ National Suicide Hotline: 1-800-SUICIDE (1-800-784-2433)

■ National Suicide Prevention Lifeline: 1-800-273-TALK

If violence or abuse is a problem:

■ National Domestic Violence/Child Abuse/Sexual Abuse: 1-800-799-SAFE

■ National Center for Victims of Crime's toll-free information and referral service: 1-800-FYI-CALL.

CHAPTER ONE

Understanding Transition Stress Reactions

This book is designed to help promote the natural recovery of those who have returned from war. You know that coming home from the war zone *physically* may take a day or days, but coming home *mentally* is a process that can take weeks or months. Your retransition from the war zone is a period for the natural and gradual process of healing to take place.

Before battle, service members are provided with training and equipment to minimize or prevent physical injuries. When you were deployed to war, you used your military training to adapt to a dangerous, foreign environment. You used what Col. Carl Castro calls your "Battlemind" to survive your hostile surroundings. Readapting to life outside of combat takes a different type of training and a different set of skills.

Resilient people have a set of tools that help them cope with and overcome the stressors in their lives. This program is designed to provide you with the training and tools you will need to retransition back from war. The transition home will be an ongoing, daily, and gradual process. Knowing what to expect puts you more in control of the recovery process.

▶ Understanding war-related stress

Our first course of action is to help you to understand some of the experiences you may be having following combat experiences. Each person's specific reactions to extreme stress will be different from other people's reactions. Some people may feel sad or numb, some may feel anxiety, and others may feel angry. Most people returning home will have a mix of many emotions, including gratitude and happiness. However, there are some types of reactions that are fairly common for people who have survived extreme situations such as a combat deployment.

■ Section A: Types of combat stress reactions

There are several types of common reactions that the body and brain have following extreme stress (Resick & Schnicke, 1993). We are going to talk about four common reactions. One type of common reaction to extreme stress is called *reexperiencing*. Reexperiencing reactions include different ways that combat events may seem to repeat in our mind or body. Reexperiencing can include upsetting memories, thoughts, and images that come into your mind, even when you are not trying to think about them, as well as dreams or nightmares about stressful events. Sometimes reexperiencing can occur when something reminds you of the stressful event. The reminders—sometimes called triggers or cues—can be many different things. Following war, a trigger may happen when veterans see certain people, when they are in places that are similar to the war zone, when they hear sounds or smell odors that remind them of their deployment. Although reexperiencing often includes thoughts, memories, and images in the mind, it also causes reactions in the body. For example, a person might experience a physical stress reaction (heart beating faster, sweating more, muscles tensing up, etc.) when something reminds them of a severely stressful event.

A second type of reaction includes the experience of being amped-up, also known as *hyperarousal*. Arousal is just energy or activation in the body. We all need some level of arousal or we could not get up and move around. Hyperarousal just means more arousal than we need, or more than is healthy or makes sense. Some veterans may feel like they have to be on guard all the time. They may startle following sudden noises and they may feel "jacked up" or "amped" a lot of the time. Some may feel very anxious or panicky. Some veterans find it hard to concentrate. They might be more irritable or angry than they used to be. Also, veterans may have trouble falling asleep or staying asleep due to hyperarousal.

The third type of reaction following extreme stress is *avoidance*. Avoidance refers to going out of our way *not* to think about or to stay away from something. Because the other reactions—reexperiencing and hyperarousal—feel bad, some veterans try to avoid reminders of their deployment or anything that might trigger these other stress reactions. If a veteran feels uncomfortable in a shopping mall, he or she might begin to avoid going to the mall. If a veteran is reminded by seeing people who remind him or her of the enemy, he or she may begin to avoid being around similar-looking types of people. Veterans might try to avoid thinking about the war zone, or talking to people about it. Some people start to keep to themselves, or avoid watching TV or reading the news.

Related to avoidance, some people may experience *emotional numbing*, or may feel depressed. This can include having a hard time relating to other people or having a hard time trusting others. Veterans with emotional numbing may feel fewer positive feelings, like happiness. Often after stressful events people have a harder time enjoying things they used to, such as hobbies or going out with other people. Sometimes veterans lose their interest in food or sex, or may not be able to function sexually. Veterans may feel guilt related to things they did or did not do, such as making it back when others did not. After combat deployment, many people feel that they just don't have as much energy as they used to, or that their memory is not as good as it used to be.

So far we have been talking specifically about deployment-related stress. However, the reactions that we have discussed are not specific to veterans. These reactions are actually common reactions to extreme stress in general. Survivors of motor vehicle accidents, natural disasters, sexual assaults, and other crimes tend to have the same types of reactions. For example, two weeks after a sexual assault, 94% of rape survivors were found to have many of these reactions (Rothbaum et al., 1992).

Remember as we talk about these reactions to stress that we are talking about normal reactions that the body and brain have to very *extreme* events. Another way to say this is that they are normal reactions to an abnormal amount of stress.

■ Section B: Stress and the brain

To help understand why you may be experiencing some of the reactions that you have had, it is very important to understand how our system—meaning our brain and body—works to deal with danger. Our system is very efficient at helping us to detect possible threats and to prepare us to deal with those threats. When we have gone through extreme stress—such as almost being killed, or seeing other people get seriously injured—our brain makes changes to become more attuned to danger. In the war zone, our system adapted to surviving in that environment. Parts of our brain actually adapt to be able to detect danger and keep you alive. Any time our brain detects possible danger it can fire the alarms and get us ready to act—to keep us safe.

The amygdala is a part of the brain's alarm system. The amygdala helps produce our emotions—including anxiety and fear (LeDoux, 2002). It is in charge of detecting danger, and then triggering the "freeze, flight, fight" system (Gray, 1988). Many of you may be familiar with the idea of fight or flight. But if we look at how our systems are really wired, the order is little different. First, when a serious threat is detected, we are wired to freeze. Freezing protects us from predatory animals that are very good at detecting movement. Second, the system is wired then to make us flee—to get away from the threat. Only when those options do not work or are impossible, are we wired to fight—as a last-ditch effort to survive. Many veterans are embarrassed if they froze or ran when attacked or were in danger in the war zone. However, this is what we are wired for! Military training works to reverse this order, but it is hard to change biology.

When we survive an extremely stressful situation, our alarm system (the amygdala) registers what is going on at the time—the temperature, the sounds we hear, the sights we can see, even the odors we smell. The amygdala registers all of these things as signs of danger. The problem is that once we are no longer in danger the amygdala interprets things we may have seen, smelled, heard, or felt as signs that danger is happening again.

When the brain detects something that it considers a sign of danger, the amygdala acts, and it acts fast. It's the amygdala's job to fire all of the alarms to the rest of the brain and body and prepare us to deal with danger. It throws adrenaline into the body, tenses the muscles, quickens the heart rate, stops digestion, and causes us to feel anxious, fearful, and on guard. Basically, it prepares us for battle. When we have survived extremely stressful or dangerous situations, the amygdala can start to be overactive. That is why when we return from war, we often feel alarmed even when we are not in danger (LeDoux, 2002).

After returning from war, the amygdala often cannot tell the difference between what is really dangerous and what is not dangerous. It cannot tell Baghdad from the basketball court, Mosul from Mom's house, or Qandahar from a candy store. It seems to forget where we are, what year it is, sometimes even who is with us. So even though hot temperatures, crowds, or enclosed places are not actually dangerous now, if you have been in dangerous situations like these in the past, the amygdala will assume you are in danger and will fire. And when it fires the "alarm," we do not just think, "maybe there's danger here." When our brain tells us something, we believe it. When the amygdala fires, we feel and believe that we are currently in danger.

After trauma, the amygdala changes our system so that the main goal is detecting danger and preparing to deal with danger. And when the system has the main goal of detecting and dealing with danger, a lot of other things fall by the wayside. The amygdala tells us "you do not need to sleep—in fact, sleeping will not keep you safe. I will keep you safe. Stay awake." It tells us "there is no need to enjoy your old activities— they will not keep you alive. No need to have a regular appetite, no need to feel close to other people, no need to feel sexual desire, no need to go out and enjoy life—those things will not keep you alive. I will keep you alive." As long as the amygdala is overactive, we can believe that we really are unsafe—no matter what is really going on.

Coming back from the combat theater, you likely feel less safe than you did at home before you left. You may take more precautions now, and feel that the world has changed. However, believing we are unsafe does not actually make us safer—in fact, it can make us less safe. We will illustrate this with an example. If you are familiar with radar systems, you may know the idea of the "signal-to-noise ratio." The signal-to-noise ratio is a measure of the amount of true information a radar detects (real threats) compared to false information, or "noise." False information (noise) is when the radar reports an object or threat when there is nothing dangerous there. Well-tuned radar will only register a threat when there is really something there— this is the optimal situation (see Figure 1.1). However, if the sensitivity of the radar is too high—maybe 1 or 2 percent—then you might get an occasional false blip. If the radar is too sensitive, we might occasionally believe there is an incoming plane and scramble to intercept it—and find nothing is there. But, if the radar system is far too overactive, you get constant blips on the radar (see Figure 1.2). Because every blip has to be investigated, we are constantly scrambling to check every signal. Of course, this is very costly. It takes too many resources to check every possible threat. We become tired, overworked, and burned out. We do not know which blip is a real threat, if there is any real threat at all. Over time, the system gets overworked to the point that if a real threat does come, it is more likely to miss it.

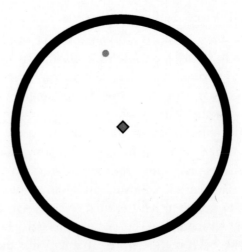

Figure 1.1 A radar system that is accurate or only slightly overactive.

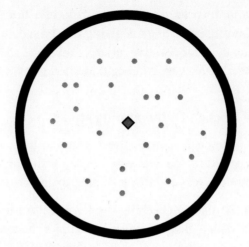

Figure 1.2 An oversensitive radar system.

■ Section C: The problem of avoidance

As mentioned previously, avoidance is when we go out of our way *not* to think about or to keep away from something. Trying to avoid reminders of highly stressful events is a natural reaction. For example, veterans who experience combat stress may try to avoid thinking about their war experiences. They may avoid talking about the war or not watch the news. However, there are a few problems with avoidance. First, there may be a lot of reminders around you, and it can be hard to avoid all the possible reminders.

There is another big problem with avoidance. Usually a lot of the things we are avoiding are things that were signs of danger in combat situations. For example, particular sounds or smells meant we needed to be ready to fight or get away quickly. The problem is that if we look at things here and now, we see that the same things we avoid are not signs of danger now. Our bodies and our brains are still avoiding cues for danger in the war zone—as if they still mean danger today.

If we avoid these reminders of the war zone, our bodies and brains do not get a chance to learn that the things that meant danger in the combat zone are not good predictors of danger here and now. When we avoid things that are not actually dangerous, we are taking away opportunities for the amygdala to learn. Even worse, the more we avoid, the more the amygdala becomes convinced that it really is dangerous.

To be able to get back to where you can go to places and enjoy doing activities you used to enjoy, you have to retrain the amygdala. There are two things that need to be done to overcome your stress reactions:

- For a while, you have to get used to the fact that even though the amygdala is firing the alarm, there really is not any real danger there.
- For a while, you will have to allow yourself to feel *uncomfortable* when your amygdala is firing. To do this, you will have to allow yourself to tolerate reminders long enough and often enough—without avoiding them—so that your amygdala can learn that nothing bad is happening.

Accurate signs of danger *do* still exist. However, the cues from the war zone are not very good ones right here, right now. Right now the main thing old reminders do is to keep us really "amped" up and uncomfortable—rather than keeping us safe. Getting better means giving the amygdala enough new training so it relearns what the cues for real danger are, and stops triggering anxiety and fear when you do not need it. Now we will begin to teach you the tools you will need to manage your stress.

■ Section D: Monitoring stress

Everyone deals with stress in his or her own way. For this reason, it is important to know how *you* deal with stress. In this section, you will learn how to measure your stress levels and to use coping tools to manage your stress in different situations.

- ■ Similar to checking the temperature in your home, we can measure stress level with a gauge. Instead of using a thermometer, the tool we use to monitor a person's stress level is the Subjective Units of Distress Scale (SUDS; Wolpe, 1973).

- ■ The scale goes from 0 to 10, with higher numbers meaning more distress. A SUDS rating of 0 is the least stress you can feel—feeling no stress at all. On the other hand, if you are at a 10, you are so stressed that you can hardly stand it.

- ■ Using the SUDS frequently is a very good way for you to know what is setting you off at a given moment in time.

- ■ If your SUDS level goes above a 5, you should use a relaxation skill to calm yourself down.

On a scale of 0–10, with 0 being the lowest amount of distress you can feel and 10 being unbearable distress or anxiety, what is your SUDS level right now? Please circle the number that fits how you feel now.

Completely Calm   **Nervous Wreck**

| 0 | 1 | 2 | 3 | 4 | 5 | 6 | 7 | 8 | 9 | 10 |

■ Section E: Relaxation skills

Now that you have noted your SUDS level, you may be aware that you are feeling stressed. There are a number of skills you can use to calm your body and mind. One is called diaphragmatic or belly breathing. Try using belly breathing any time you feel upset, tense, or stressed out. With practice, it can help relax your body and distract you from what is bothering you.

Take some time now to try the relaxation skill below.

Diaphragmatic (belly) breathing

Something as simple as the way we breathe can help reduce stress. In general, we can say that most people do not breathe properly. We tend to rush our breathing, taking shallow breaths, from the chest. This is not an effective way of breathing. And when we get really stressed, we might even hyperventilate.

Have you ever noticed babies while they are sleeping? How do they breathe? When babies breathe in, their stomachs come out. When they exhale, their stomachs go flat. That is the proper way of breathing. As we get older and deal with life stress, we reverse the process. Adults usually breathe too shallow and too fast. What we want to do is to slow down our breathing to relax and to help our bodies be more efficient and not get overworked.

We are now going to teach a skill called diaphragmatic (belly) breathing. Belly breathing is a great tool to make us feel relaxed and calm. It helps our bodies to slow down and get more oxygen. This bodily change maximizes both our physical and mental abilities, so that we perform at our best. Best of all, belly breathing is very easy, quick, and useful in any situation. You don't need any equipment, and you can do it anywhere, practically anytime.

Before practicing belly breathing for a few minutes, please take a moment to write your SUDS level before you start (see Figure 1.3):

SUDS: Before relaxation: _____/ 10

To practice belly breathing, sit comfortably in your chair with your hands resting on your stomach and your fingers laced together. Go ahead and take a nice deep breath in. As you do this, your stomach will come out and expand. Hold it for as long as it is comfortable. Then exhale very slowly—as you do, your belly will go back in and deflate. You can think of it as inhaling and filling your belly like a balloon gets filled with air—holding it for a few seconds, and then very slowly letting the air out of the balloon so that it deflates again. This may seem uncomfortable at first, but with a little practice it becomes a very useful relaxation skill.

If you want to, you can close your eyes and take a deep breath in, so your belly expands—hold for a few seconds—and then slowly exhale, so your belly goes in again. Then take another slow breath. Now, please practice belly breathing for at least three minutes. After three minutes, you should feel more relaxed. If you do not feel more relaxed, keep trying. Some people need a while to get the hang of it.

Now that you have practiced belly breathing, please take just a moment again to note your SUDS—estimating your level of distress on the scale from 0 to 10. Write down your number here:

SUDS: After relaxation: _____/ 10

Hopefully you saw a decrease. If it's not that much of a decrease, do not be alarmed. It takes practice to get the numbers down. It is a skill that needs to be developed over time. Once you get it, you will know it—because you will feel much better.

Figure 1.3   Subjective Units of Distress Scale (SUDS).

■ Section F: Treatments for transition stress reactions

It is possible that you or someone you know is experiencing frequent nightmares, unwanted and distressing thoughts, images, or memories, hypervigilance, anxiety, depression, difficulty feeling positive emotions, or feeling very angry. If you are having any of these experiences, please know there is help available.

One of the most common treatments for these concerns is cognitive-behavioral treatment with a professional who is trained in dealing with stress reactions. A trained mental health professional helps to discover what might be setting off these reactions. He or she would then provide clear ways of dealing with these problems. It can also be very helpful to work with a primary care physician or psychiatrist who can prescribe medication to help ease some of the symptoms.

▶ When to talk to your doctor

Have you or someone you know been:

- Avoiding people much of the time?
- Using drugs or alcohol more than normal or using them as an attempt to numb the pain inside or as the only way to relax or sleep?
- Feeling overwhelmed by your symptoms?
- Thinking of hurting yourself or someone else?

Did you answer YES to ONE or more of these questions? If so, talk to your doctor right away.

▶ The heart of the matter

The transition from the war zone will be an ongoing, daily, gradual process. In this book, we provide you with the skills you will need to deal with reactions some people experience following war. We help you begin a plan of action so that you can be better prepared to cope with the transition back into civilian life. Use the SUDS to measure your stress level at least once per day. Then practice your new relaxation skills daily as well.

- Please turn to the end of the chapter and take the quiz. The quizzes are a good way to review some of the important points in the chapter.

▶ On your own

In the week ahead, try practicing belly breathing when you notice your stress level increasing. Take note of your SUDS level, then practice belly breathing for at least three minutes, then note your SUDS level. With practice, this relaxation tool will become more effective.

Additionally, isolating yourself from other people means losing support, friendship, and closeness with others, and more time to worry or feel hopeless and alone. Many veterans tend to isolate from other people to help avoid the reminders and stress that goes along with talking to people. However, support from other people is one of the most important things to help you cope with combat stress. Therefore, one of the tools we will expect you to use is the telephone.

We would like for you to make phone calls to others in the week ahead, to help you connect with other people. Complete the Phone Calling Exercise, in which you call other people you know. Take the opportunity to talk to the other person for a few minutes.

Phone Calling Exercise

1. If you are part of a treatment group and were assigned a question, then follow the suggestions from your group leader. Ask your question when you call each group member, and note each person's response. Remember that you should only ask your question if you initiated the phone call. When you receive a call, it is fine to call the other person right back after you have hung up.

2. If you are not part of a treatment group, set a goal for yourself to call five or more people in the next week. The phone calls can be to people that you frequently talk to, or to people that you have not talked to much recently. When you start practicing with this exercise, if it is more comfortable for you, you might call for a specific reason—such as asking about details for an upcoming event. As time goes by you may feel more comfortable making more calls. The important thing right now is to start reaching out by making phone calls to other people.

3. Using the Phone Calling Exercise Worksheet, write down your own SUDS before and after each call, as well as how long you are on the phone during each call.

4. Begin to practice, using your belly breathing skills at least once a day during the coming week. Find a quiet place where you will not be disturbed. At first it is best to practice these skills when you are already feeling relatively calm. Like any other skill, it is hard to learn it under stress, so practice when you do not need it at first. As you get better at using these skills, you will be able to use them more and more, even under higher stress.

Remember that learning any new skill means taking the time and energy to practice and focus on learning. Also, as with trying anything new, it may feel a little weird at first. Keep practicing. Like many other skills you have practiced and gotten good at, with time you will get better and better. As you master each of the tools we provide in the workbook, they become easier to use, and more useful.

Phone Calling Exercise

Name: _____

Session Number: _____

Question: _____

Person Called	Date	Your Own SUDS Before (0–10)	Answer/Topic	Call Length	Your Own SUDS After (0–10)

Name: _____

Date: _____ _____ / _____ _____ / _____ _____

1. What term refers to going out of our way *not* to think about, or to keep away from something:
    a. Hypervigilance
    b. Avoidance
    c. Reexperiencing
    d. Dropping out

2. It's very unusual to experience unwanted memories after returning from the war zone.
    True or False

3. Although reminders of stressful combat events can feel overwhelming, the reaction to reminders often lessens with time.
    True or False

4. Isolating from other people means loss of support, friendship, and closeness with others, and more time to worry or feel hopeless and alone.
    True or False

5. What does SUDS stand for?
    a. Strong Underpinnings of Denial and Suppression
    b. Subjective Units of Distress Scale
    c. The stuff you find floating at the top of beer
    d. Soapscum Under Da Sink

6. Working all the time to try to avoid distressing memories of the stressful event is a good way to deal with post-war stress.
    True or False

Managing Stress

When an individual undergoes stress over time, consistent, long-term changes occur in both the brain and the body. Long-term stress that is not managed can lead to changes in certain chemicals in the brain and interfere with optimal, healthy functioning. This means that a person under stress would have a more difficult time dealing with additional stress. Thus, managing stress is extremely important, particularly for veterans who are transitioning from the war zone.

In this chapter, we provide a review of common stress reactions, and describe positive and negative ways of coping with stress. We discuss the importance of monitoring one's level of stress, and teach positive ways of dealing with that stress.

■ Section A: Unmanaged stress

When human beings endure too much stress and do not manage it, the effects can be physical, emotional, and mental. For example, it is common for people returning from war to feel physically, mentally, and emotionally "on guard" and ready to take on anything dangerous.

Some common physical symptoms of stress include:

- Rapid heartbeat
- Headache
- Stiff neck and/or tight shoulders
- Backache
- Rapid breathing
- Sweating and sweaty palms
- Upset stomach, nausea, or diarrhea

Some common feelings and emotional symptoms of stress include:

- Feeling easily irritated or frustrated
- Losing your temper and yelling at others for no reason
- Feeling jumpy
- Being exhausted all the time
- Feeling ashamed or guilty
- Feeling anxious or worried

Some common symptoms of stress include:

- Finding it hard to concentrate or focus on tasks
- Thinking too much about insignificant things
- Doubting your ability to do things
- Having problems remembering things
- Believing you are missing opportunities because you cannot act quickly

Below, you will find the Identifying Stress Cues Worksheet. Please take a moment and fill it out. This will help you understand how you respond to stress.

Identifying Stress Cues Worksheet

A very important part of monitoring our stress is to identify how we react to things that happen in our lives. These are cues because, if we pay attention to them, we will be able to know that we are in a high-stress situation. Please fill out each section so that you can become more aware of what your own particular stress cues are, and what sets you off and stresses you out.

1. Physical cues (how your body responds to stress; i.e., increased heart rate, tightness in chest, upset stomach, feeling hot):

   _____

   _____

   _____

2. Feeling and emotional cues (feelings that come up; i.e., fear, anger, sadness, guilt):

   _____

   _____

   _____

3. Thinking and mental cues (what we think about in response to the event; i.e., negative self-talk such as "I'm going to lose control," "I've got to get out of here," "I can't handle this"):

   _____

   _____

   _____

It is common for veterans to return from their service in-country feeling amped or on-guard most of the time. And of course it is important to be able to develop this kind of mode—while you were in-country, you absolutely needed to stay "on" most, if not all, of the time. Your safety, your life, and the lives of others around you relied on your being ready for anything to happen. We often believe that being hypervigilant—that is, keeping a high level of alertness—is essential to keep us safe. We tell

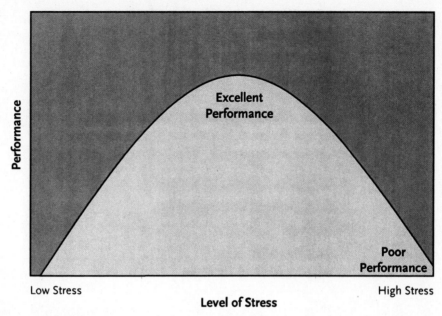

Figure 2.1   We perform best at a medium level of stress. With too little stress, we may not be motivated, but too much stress interferes with our functioning.

ourselves that staying all the way keyed-up makes it more likely that we will be able to respond to whatever situation comes up.

In the last section, we discussed the reality that a moderate level of arousal is more efficient and safer than hyperarousal. The same is true for stress (see Figure 2.1). Although a moderate level of stress helps us to handle situations, once our stress level gets too high, we are actually *less* ready to handle difficult situations. As you can see in Figure 2.1, when we have a moderate level of stress, we are at our peak physically, emotionally, and mentally.

When our body is too amped up, we miss important details, misinterpret situations, make poor judgments, and perform less well. Also, over time stress wears us out, and makes it less likely that we will be able to respond to situations accurately and quickly. Over a long period of time, stress wears down our body and weakens our immune systems, making us more likely to get a number of diseases. Once the initial threat is over (i.e., after a deployment), we have a choice. It is much healthier and safer for us to bring our overall stress level down.

■ Section B: Coping with and managing stress

There are a number of ways to manage your stress. You already learned how to identify how stressed you feel (e.g., with SUDS, described in Chapter 1 and the Identifying Stress Cues Worksheet in this chapter). Now we are going to discuss some of the most important tools that you can use to de-stress. These are mind-centered and body-centered exercises. *Mind-centered exercises* are stress management skills that focus on calming your mind. Some mind-centered exercises include:

■ Meditation (including mindfulness meditation)
■ Prayer

- Visualization
- Self-hypnosis
- Autogenic training
- Music therapy

Each of these skills can be used to help calm your mind, which can also relax your body and decrease your stress. There are a number of *body-centered exercises,* which are stress management skills focused on your body. These include:

- Diaphragmatic (belly) breathing
- Progressive muscle relaxation
- Massage
- Aromatherapy
- Yoga, Tai Chi, or Qi Gong

These exercises calm your body and your emotions. They are very useful skills to help you to feel more relaxed and less stressed.

Now let's try another body-centered exercise. First, on a scale of 0–10, with 0 being the lowest amount of distress you can feel and 10 being unbearable distress or anxiety, what is your SUDS level right now? Please circle the number that fits how you feel now (see Figure 2.2).

Here is another example of a relaxation tool called Progressive Muscle Relaxation (or PMR). Try using PMR breathing at least once a day to help keep your stress level down. With practice, it can help relax your body and promote better functioning. Begin by lying on your back or sitting in your chair in a comfortable position.

- If you are lying down, allow your arms to rest at your sides, palms down, on the surface next to you. If you are sitting, rest your hands on your lap.
- Inhale and exhale slowly and deeply.
- Clench your hands into fists and hold them tightly for 15 seconds. As you do this, relax the rest of your body. Visualize your fists contracting, becoming tighter and tighter.
- Then let your hands relax. On relaxing, see a golden light (like the sun) flowing into the entire body, making all your muscles soft and pliable.
- Now, tense and relax the following parts of your body in this order: face, shoulders, back, stomach, pelvis, legs, feet, and toes. Hold each part tensed for 15 seconds and then relax your body for 30 seconds before going on to the next part.
- Finish the exercise by shaking your hands and imagining the remaining tension flowing out of your fingertips.

Figure 2.2 Subjective Units of Distress Scale (SUDS).

Now take another moment to note your SUDS level after having practiced this skill. Does your body feel more relaxed? How much more relaxed? How much calmer do you feel afterward?

Completely Calm   **Nervous Wreck**

| | | | | | | | | | | |
0   1   2   3   4   5   6   7   8   9   10

Skills improve with practice. Relaxation is no different. We must practice the skills to perfect them—to be able to automatically recall them when we need them most—such as when we are really stressed out. A perfect example is when we learn self-defense or combat tactics. The more you practice them, the more they become ingrained, so that you can recall them instantly in a time of need. The same holds true for relaxation therapies. They should be practiced often for their usefulness in producing helpful and lasting results. Remember that like any new skill or way of doing things, it may feel funny or strange at first when you practice these relaxation skills. Remind yourself that the feeling of strangeness will decrease as you practice it, and your ability will increase. Stick with it long enough so that you become skilled, so that you will feel more relaxed and in control of your body's reactions.

■ Section C: Treatments for stress and anxiety

Treatments for anxiety and stress generally start with examining what causes a person to feel stressed or anxious. Once the cause(s) of stress are identified, the person can then work with his or her mental health professional and doctor to identify the best way(s) to manage that stress. Common treatments for managing stress include: biofeedback, body awareness training, and the other coping skills we talked about in this chapter. If you are unable to reduce your stress using the skills in the chapter, consider seeing your doctor. Some medications may also be helpful to help calm that anxiety in the short run.

▶ When to talk to your doctor

Have you or someone you know been:

- Experiencing your heart racing, headaches, backaches, or having an upset stomach pretty frequently?
- Feeling exhausted or overwhelmed?
- Feeling like you might hurt yourself or someone else?

Did you answer YES to ONE or more of these questions? If so, talk to your doctor right away.

▶ **The heart of the matter**

In this chapter, we spoke about common stress reactions that you may be experiencing now—since returning from war. There are both positive and negative coping reactions to stress. It is important that we check ourselves and monitor our stress levels. One way of doing this is by using the SUDS level to measure distress at least one time per day. By monitoring our stress and knowing what triggers us, we are more apt to use positive coping to deal with that stress. There are numerous body-centered and mind-centered ways of improving the ways that we manage stress. As with any new skill, relaxation skills need to be practiced again and again, so that we can remember how to use them when we need to.

■ Please turn to the end of the chapter and take the quiz. Remember that the quizzes are a good way to review some of the important points in the chapter.

▶ **On your own**

1. Complete the Phone Calling Exercise Worksheet in the same way that you did for the last session. Remember to note your SUDS before and after each call. Complete details about this exercise are included in the On Your Own section at the end of Chapter 1.

2. Use the Weekly Stress Monitoring Worksheet so you can know what sets you off and increases your stress. Awareness is key to producing changes.

3. Practice PMR and belly breathing at least one time per day in the next week. Write down what days and times you are able to practice that skill on the Weekly Stress Management Schedule at the end of this chapter.

You are on your way to managing your stress level! Remember, you must practice these skills every day to keep your stress level down. Any time you feel guilty about taking the time to do this, remember that *your effort will be worth it.*

Phone Calling Exercise Workksheet

Name: _____

Session Number: _____

Question: _____

Person Called	Date	Your Own SUDS Before (0–10)	Answer/Topic	Call Length	Your Own SUDS After (0–10)

Weekly Stress Monitoring Worksheet

Use this sheet to record your stress during the week. You can still use this worksheet in session to discuss what occurred that caused your stress to rise, and what you did to manage the stress reaction. This can also be used to help you develop additional strategies to deal with similar situations in the future.

1. For each day this week, monitor and record the highest number you reach on the Stress Meter.

    _____ Monday

    _____ Tuesday

    _____ Wednesday

    _____ Thursday

    _____ Friday

    _____ Saturday

    _____ Sunday

2. What was the highest number you reached on the Stress Meter during the week?

    _____ / 10

3. What type of events triggered your stress?

    _____

    _____

4. What cues were associated with the stress-inducing event?

    Physical Cues _____

    _____

    _____

    Feeling Cues _____

    _____

    _____

    Thinking Cues _____

    _____

    _____

5. What strategies did you use to prevent hitting a 10 on the Stress Meter (assuming you did not hit a 10)?

    _____

    _____

Stress Management Schedule

Write down what times you will practice at least one stress management skill in the week ahead. Try to practice at least one technique per day. Put this schedule some place in your home where you will see it often—such as your refrigerator door, bathroom mirror, or nightstand.

	Monday	Tuesday	Wednesday	Thursday	Friday	Saturday	Sunday
0600 hrs.							
0700 hrs.							
0800 hrs.							
0900 hrs.							
1000 hrs.							
1100 hrs.							
1200 hrs.							
1300 hrs.							
1400 hrs.							
1500 hrs.							
1600 hrs.							
1700 hrs.							
1800 hrs.							
1900 hrs.							
2000 hrs.							
2100 hrs.							
2200 hrs.							
Night ↓							

▶ **Chapter 2—Stress management quiz**

Name: _____

Date: _____ _____ / _____ _____ / _____ _____

1. What are some common symptoms of long-term stress?
   a. Irritability
   b. Upset stomach, nausea, diarrhea
   c. Stiff neck or headaches
   d. All of these are common

2. Which of these are **positive ways** to cope with stress?
   a. Exercise
   b. Driving fast in your car
   c. Drinking a case of beer
   d. All of these are a positive way to cope with stress

3. Which of these are **negative ways** to cope with stress?
   a. Obsessing or worrying about things
   b. Smoking marijuana
   c. Road raging
   d. All of these are not good

4. What would be an example of a **mind-centered** stress management skill?
   a. Guided imagery
   b. Self-hypnosis
   c. Autogenics
   d. All of these are mind-centered skills

5. This is a relaxation skill where you breathe in with your belly coming out, and exhaling and your belly coming back in. It is very easy and helps people to relax. What is it called?
   a. Autoreflex breathing
   b. Deep muscle breathing
   c. Diaphragmatic breathing
   d. Exhalation Therapy

CHAPTER THREE

Tools for Healthy Coping

In this session, we will talk about and develop a plan to start using healthy coping activities that help people build their own resilience. These coping tools will help us become better able to deal with the effects of stressful events and continue a healthy recovery. Healthy coping activities are different for different individuals, but all of them help people to tolerate stress reactions and decrease the risk for depression. It is important to stay active in addressing problems as they come up—when we take direct action to cope with our problems, we keep ourselves in a position of power so that we feel stronger and less helpless.

■ Section A: Reactive and proactive coping tools

First of all, let's talk about coping strategies. There are two types of tools that are important in an overall plan for effective coping:

- *Reactive coping tools* are skills and behaviors that we do in response to a problem. Like firefighters responding to a fire in progress, reactive strategies are focused on reducing or removing a problem that is already there. If you are stressed and use belly breathing to help calm yourself down, you are using a reactive coping tool.

- *Proactive coping tools* are behaviors that we do to prevent problems from taking place or to prepare ourselves to better handle possible problems that might occur in the future. These include skills and habits that improve our overall health, making us more capable of handling stresses in general. This also includes practicing and mastering skills when we do not immediately need them (for example, practicing relaxation skills when you're already feeling pretty relaxed) so that we get better and can use the skill when we most need them (and when they are hardest to use). Many of the skills and activities that we will discuss in this chapter are proactive coping skills.

People vary in the ways they deal with stress. This is called one's *coping style*. Some people can be more prone to take action in times of stress; others tend to be very reflective and study the situation. And others tend to become reserved, not doing much in times of stress.

Similarly, different people enjoy different kinds of activities. Some people like walking in the woods, others like wild parties with lots of people. Some people like building models or working on engines, while others like taking pictures or painting landscapes. Others like running, or working out. When it comes to healing and re-adapting to being back home, the best healthy coping behavior is the one that you will make a commitment to doing on a regular basis.

In the following section, we explore the importance of healthy coping activities. We also look at types of activities that are especially likely to make people feel good. We start by describing how *not* engaging in coping activities can lead to negative outcomes, such as depression.

■ Section B: Depression and the danger of doing nothing

Over the years, researchers have studied why people feel depressed and what drives depression for various individuals. For example, some studies have shown that when someone has negative thoughts, he or she is more likely to become depressed (Seligman, 1991). Studies also conclude that when people focus too much on themselves and blame themselves for their problems, they have more depression.

When we have negative thoughts that automatically pop up in our minds, this can lead to negative feelings such as sadness or anger. And these thoughts and feelings can lead to negative beliefs about other people, our futures, and ourselves. Negative thoughts, feelings, and beliefs also all lead to depression (Beck, 1995). We know—based on research—that negativity can breed more negativity, and this can be a vicious cycle for a person. In fact, it can lead to a "downward spiral of depression," (Lewinsohn et al., 1985) which means that someone who thinks, feels, and believes in a very negative way will feed negativity, and they will become more and more depressed over time (see Figure 3.1). Basically, this is what can happen:

- When people have depressed *feelings,* they may have discouraging *thoughts,* and are less likely to do the things (engage in *behavior*) that might make them feel better. This leads to even greater depression, which in turn leads to more discouraging thoughts that then lead to more inactivity.

- Additionally, war injuries and/or chronic pain may be keeping us from doing the kinds of activities we used to do to have fun or to feel better.

- When we are doing very few activities, we are more likely to feel depressed. Also, when we feel depressed, we do not feel like doing the kinds of activities that are likely to help us out of depression.

Figure 3.1 Interactions among thoughts, feelings, and behavior.

- When we are depressed or feeling out of sorts, we are least likely to do the things that we need the most—the things that are most likely to help us feel better. This is known as the *downward spiral of depression* (see Figure 3.2). It becomes a dangerous, vicious, negative spiral.

Depression keeps us from doing activities that once were fun and healthy for us. Physical injuries may make it even harder for us to do things we used to enjoy. However, the less we do, the more depressed we feel. The more depressed we feel, the less we feel like doing anything.

■ Section C: Negative coping, negative mood

Some things that people do to try to cope can actually make their mood worse. These *negative coping responses* can be anything that does not bring us what is really

Bob feels
discouraged

Bob thinks
"I am useless"

Bob doesn't
go out

Bob feels
depressed

Bob thinks
"Nobody cares"

Bob stays in
all week

Bob feels
more suicidal

Figure 3.2   The downward spiral of depression.

good for us in the long run. Even though we might be doing these coping activities to try to feel better, the reality is that people who use negative ways of coping usually feel worse. They usually feel angrier, more upset, and more depressed. Here are examples of negative coping responses:

- Criticizing yourself (negative self-talk)
- Driving too fast in your car
- Becoming aggressive or violent (hitting someone, throwing, or kicking something)
- Eating too much or too little, or drinking a lot of caffeinated beverages
- Smoking or chewing tobacco
- Drinking alcohol or taking recreational drugs
- Yelling at your spouse or partner, children, coworkers, or friends
- Avoiding social contact
- Dropping out of recreational activities
- Working long hours to avoid thoughts or people

Negative coping behaviors can lead to a downward spiral. Fortunately the opposite is also true—there is also a *positive spiral*. The more positive coping we do, the less depressed we feel, and the less depressed we feel, the more we will feel able to do things. Getting your post-deployment life back on track will involve making the effort to start doing the things that will break the downward spiral.

■ Section D: Positive action, positive mood

Positive coping behaviors break the downward spiral by helping individuals to do more activities that are going to improve their mood. And as people begin to incorporate more of these positive behaviors into their life, the positive coping begins to make them feel better, and to give them more energy. So in addition to beginning to feel better, it also becomes easier to do more positive behaviors, and the benefits begin to multiply.

Again, our goal is to begin practicing more activities that result in decreased stress and anxiety, as well as better overall mood and better overall health. Even if you are having trouble enjoying the activities at first, these activities help to move you towards a better mood and better energy—and being able to continue with more positive coping habits. This can help to create a pattern of healthy improvement, rather than continuing decline. Here are some positive ways of dealing with stress and promoting better health and coping:

Positive Coping Responses

- Playing with children, your spouse or partner, or a pet
- Writing, painting, or other creative activity
- Praying or going to church
- Exercising or getting outdoors to enjoy nature
- Listening to positive music

- Laughing or crying
- Going out with a friend (playing golf, going to a movie, going bowling, going out to dinner)
- Taking a relaxing bath or shower
- Discussing situations with a spouse or partner, or close friend
- Gardening or making home repairs
- Singing or dancing
- Practicing deep breathing, meditation, or progressive muscle relaxation

Types of positive coping activities

Now we are going to get more specific. In this section, we provide you with a summary of three categories of things you can do to help you feel better—things that will help prevent stress and depression.

Category one: Body-focused activities

Body-focused activities can be a great way to decrease levels of stress and depression and increase energy. Many of these exercises reduce chemicals in the body associated with stress and increase chemicals that produce good feelings, helping to promote overall good health and mood.

Mind/Body exercises focus on helping the body to better handle stress. They are all focused on relaxing or focusing our energy in a more positive and healthy way, or both.

Physical Exercise

- Going for a walk
- Bicycle riding
- Swimming
- Lifting weights
- Hiking
- Playing a sport with someone
- Kayaking
- Surfing
- Jogging or running
- Doing yardwork
- Cleaning house

Mind/Body Exercises

- Diaphragmatic/belly breathing
- Progressive muscle relaxation
- Massage
- Aromatherapy

- Yoga
- Tai Chi
- Qi Gong
- Meditation
- Pilates
- Autogenics
- Hypnosis

Category two: Goal-focused activities

We all need to feel useful and productive. Setting positive goals and achieving them is an excellent way to improve mood and decrease depression. Achieving something can include:

- Learning a new skill
- Starting on a new project
- Cleaning out the closet
- Organizing your bills
- Planning an event
- Solving a problem at-hand
- Fixing something that is broken
- Taking a class
- Learning a new language
- Learning to play an instrument

Category three: Social activities

As we have discussed, often following highly stressful events, such as military deployments, people are inclined to isolate themselves from others. However, resisting this urge to isolate and instead increasing social activities provides us with support. Being with others also helps our brain and bodies begin to re-regulate and readapt to being back home—social activity is good for the brain. Also, social activities create more opportunities for us to experience positive interactions with others.

- *Talking with others:* Call family members or talk to a close friend who you trust. Talking with a person with whom you feel safe (a family member, friend, spouse or partner, clergy, therapist, etc.) helps us feel understood, and it helps us see things a little differently sometimes.

- *Spending time with others:* Join a social club, invite someone over, have coffee or play cards with your friends, play a team sport, go to a party, make new friends, take someone on a date, play with a pet, or just sit and watch other people.

- *Helping others:* Volunteer to help others, such as at a hospital, nursing home, soup kitchen, or homeless shelter. Help friends or family members, visit someone who is lonely, spend time with children or the elderly, or help organize or coach a team. When we provide service to others, it can help us to focus our mind on positive action and can help others accomplish things they could not have done otherwise.

Category four: Other positive activities

There are numerous other activities that have been shown to help reduce stress and promote better health and better mood. Some other examples include:

- *Writing or journaling:* Writing letters, stories, poetry, or writing in a journal can help improve well-being and lower people's risk for disease. Writing 10–15 minutes a day about stress in your life especially can lower your stress level quite a bit.

- *Going out:* Plan a trip, take a drive, go fishing, go to a concert, a fair, the zoo, a restaurant, a park, a museum, or to the beach.

- *Laughing and crying:* Laughing and crying are natural ways to relieve stress and release tension. They are both part of the emotional healing process. Tell a joke, laugh at a comedy, or cry during sad movies. All of these can be excellent ways to help release stress. Even though we often think that we should not cry, or that it is a sign of weakness, the reality is that crying is an important and natural part of the overall grieving process, and can be part of getting better.

- *Create something:* Draw a picture, paint a painting, write or play music, make crafts, do yard work, or decorate your house.

- *Try a hobby:* Build a model, take up photography, learn to cook, read a book, collect baseball cards, or do something that is meaningful to you.

- *Be spiritual:* Pray, join a house of worship, talk with others about ethics or religion, go to a religious service, read sacred works, listen to a sermon, or participate in church groups.

- *Do something fun:* Go boating, hiking, camping, swimming, diving, toss a ball or a Frisbee, play chess, checkers, dominoes, or another game, or go shopping.

- *Relax:* Relax somewhere that makes you feel peaceful, take a walk, go to the woods, daydream, watch a sunset, go to the library, listen to the radio or to the sound of the ocean or a running brook.

Choose one activity from each category above that you might be able to do in the next week.

■ Section E: Common pitfalls

There are several common challenges that people frequently encounter. It is important to recognize and be ready to confront these challenges, so that they do not interfere with healthy coping.

Feeling numb

Following a deployment, some veterans report feeling like nothing is fun or enjoyable anymore. Remember that the positive spiral can be a slow process. When you start doing an activity, it is likely to feel sort of flat—not fun or rewarding at first. It may be this way for a while. However, over time, positive activities help boost our mood—this also makes it easer for our motivation to increase, making it easier to do the activities. Even better, the activities become more enjoyable. But it takes time and practice.

Avoidance

Remember from Chapter 1 that people returning from the war zone will often avoid activities and reminders of deployment. They may also avoid doing things that were related to danger in a war zone, but that will not really lead to danger back home. For example, some people may avoid driving, being in crowds, or simply sitting in the middle of a movie theater because it triggers reminders of danger. Because the brain and body adjust to dangerous situations, after stress, it is important to help our bodies learn the difference between what is dangerous and what is merely uncomfortable. The only way to do this is to practice being active again. We have to give ourselves the chance to relearn that most activities are safe.

Having no motivation

When we are depressed, we are least likely to do the things that we need the most to keep our lives on track. Depression makes it difficult to motivate ourselves to do the things we need to do: clean the house, pay our bills, or play with our children. However, all of these activities make people feel useful, capable, and independent. Making ourselves complete a task (such as running an errand, organizing a project, doing a job well, or learning something new) will actually help prevent the downward spiral of depression.

Injuries

Injuries or chronic pain may keep you from doing the same types of activities that used to be fun or rewarding. *But it is very important not to let that stop you!* Again, when you first start doing an activity, it is likely to not be fun or rewarding at first. It may be this way for a while. Additionally, it may take some time to find new activities. One veteran, for example, was in a wheelchair and was no longer able to play catch with his 10-year-old son, as he used to. Rather than give up the game, this man brought out his 7-year-old to help. His younger child caught the ball for him, and then the veteran threw it back to his older son.

Life changes

Changes in life—including relocation—may also keep you from doing the exact types of activities you used to do. Again, it may take some real creativity and problem-solving skill to find new activities that are rewarding for you. For example, a veteran loved to mountain bike. However, she was now stationed somewhere with no mountains. Rather than give up biking, she bought a racing bike and started taking bike tours a few times a week. Although at first she missed mountain biking, over time the new activity replaced mountain biking and became just as much fun.

■ Section F: Putting coping activities in action

1. Choose one positive coping activity that you want or need to do in the next week.

2. How can you make sure you accomplish this activity? Break the activity down into smaller steps. For example, let's say you have gotten behind in your house cleaning and do not have any motivation to clean. You may set a goal to spend 15 minutes a day this week cleaning your home. One day you can do a load of laundry. The next day you can put all your clothes away. The next you can vacuum the bedroom.

3. Identify which days and times you will complete the activity next to the activity, write down how long—and how often—you would be willing to do the activity.

A NOTE ABOUT GRIEF

Grief is a normal and natural response to loss, but if neglected can affect you in ways that you may not notice at first. Because talking about losses and death is often awkward and uncomfortable, veterans suffering from grief often avoid dealing with their thoughts and feelings related to loss. If you are having high levels of grief or guilt, we urge you to talk to your chaplain or a mental health professional.

■ Section G: Treatments for transition stress

As mentioned in Chapter 1, one of the most common treatments for transition stress reactions is cognitive-behavioral treatment with a professional who is trained in dealing with these concerns. If you are bothered by reactions like the ones we have been discussing, it may be useful for you to work with a trained mental health professional on ways to deal with these reactions. It may also be useful to work with a primary care physician or psychiatrist who can prescribe medication to help ease some of the symptoms. Medications can help neurochemicals in the brain to readjust to healthier levels, which can help you to reduce your anxiety as well as help to manage your reactions to things.

▶ When to talk to your doctor

Have you or someone you know been:

- Feeling very depressed and discouraged?
- Using drugs or alcohol more than normal, or using them as an attempt to numb the pain inside, or as the only way to relax or sleep?

- Feeling overwhelmed by your symptoms?
- Thinking of hurting yourself or someone else?

Did you answer YES to ONE or more of these questions? If so, talk to your doctor right away.

▶ The heart of the matter

The transition from the war zone will be an ongoing, daily, gradual process. In this section, we provide you with the tools you will need to deal with reactions some people experience following war. We help you begin a plan of action so that you can be better prepared to cope with the transition back into civilian life. Specifically, we encourage you to use several types of activities that promote good feelings and help ward off depression, such as positive body-focused activities, goal-focused activities, and positive social activities. These activities will promote better mood and better overall health. We encourage use of these healthy coping behaviors on a regular basis. Engaging in these healthy coping activities will help promote the upward spiral of recovery.

- Please turn to the end of the chapter and take the quiz. Remember that the quizzes are a good way to review some of the important points in the chapter.

▶ On your own

1. Complete the Phone Calling Exercise Worksheet in the same way that you did for the last session. Remember to note your SUDS before and after each call.

2. On your own, we would like you to look over the list of healthy coping activities in this chapter. Identify one activity from each of the four categories (body-focused activities, goal-focused activities, social activities, and other positive activities) that you are willing to do in the week ahead. By reviewing these activities and even adding similar activities to these lists, you will eventually be able to select a number of coping activities to participate in to increase your resilience.

3. Use the Coping Activity Schedule at the end of this chapter to write down the days and times that you plan to engage in at least one positive coping activity per day. For example, maybe you would like to choose swimming as an activity. You could write down and schedule yourself to go swimming for 30 minutes, three times per week on Mondays, Wednesdays, and Fridays.

Here are two examples of how other veterans planned to participate in coping activities:

Joe Is a Father of Two Who Works as a Project Manager

- For day one, Joe planned to go to his favorite take-out restaurant and have a lunch he really enjoyed.
- He intended to focus on learning a new computer program that he's been meaning to become skilled at, and that he enjoys doing, for 15 minutes each day.
- He planned to spend an hour playing with his kids in the yard when he gets home.

Dennis Is a Single 18-Year-Old Who Works as an Airplane Mechanic

- For his plan, Dennis chose to call a favorite buddy that he used to work with, but who now works in another building, and to say hi during his lunch break.

- Because he enjoys inspecting and caring for planes, he planned to challenge himself at work by seeing how quickly and efficiently he could complete the inspections he was required to do every morning.

- He also planned to rent a comedy dvd Friday night that would get him laughing.

After returning from an experience as profound as war, it can be very difficult to get back into habits that will keep you healthy and help you cope with problems. When too many serious problems are happening, it is hard to remember to take time for yourself. Sometimes we feel we do not have any more energy. But taking time for healthy coping activities is important. It is really important at this time to fight against the urge to "veg out" or to turn to other negative coping habits. It may take some time, and it may not even feel like fun at first. Reversing the downward spiral takes extra effort. Making these activities a part of your daily lifestyle is an important first step toward healing.

Phone Calling Exercise Worksheet

Name: _____

Session Number: _____

Question: _____

Person Called	Date	Your Own SUDS Before (0–10)	Answer/Topic	Call Length	Your Own SUDS After (0–10)

▶ Coping activities schedule

We need to develop a plan of action to help us cope with the transition from the war zone. We may not feel interested in the kinds of activities that we used to think were fun. Injuries and chronic pain may make us unable to do the kinds of activities we used to that kept us at our best. Therefore, we have to identify new activities, and make the time to do something fun every day.

Use the Coping Activities Schedule to write down times when you can do a healthy coping activity from ideas in this chapter. Try to make time for at least three activities per day. Put this schedule in a place in your home where you will see it often, such as on your refrigerator door or bathroom mirror.

Coping Activities Schedule

	Monday	Tuesday	Wednesday	Thursday	Friday	Saturday	Sunday
0600 hrs.							
0700 hrs.							
0800 hrs.							
0900 hrs.							
1000 hrs.							
1100 hrs.							
1200 hrs.							
1300 hrs.							
1400 hrs.							
1500 hrs.							
1600 hrs.							
1700 hrs.							
1800 hrs.							
1900 hrs.							
2000 hrs.							
2100 hrs.							
2200 hrs.							
Night ↓							

Name: _____

Date: _____ _____ / _____ _____ / _____ _____

1. Reactive coping tools are behaviors that we use to prepare ourselves for problems that might occur in the future.

   True or False

2. Social isolation helps protect a person from problems and is a good way to help a person adjust to being back home after a deployment.

   True or False

3. Setting and achieving goals is an important way to improve mood and decrease depression.

   True or False

4. When a person feels anxious in a situation that used to be comfortable, it means that he or she should get out of that situation as quickly as possible and avoid that situation in the future.

   True or False

5. As soon as we start doing pleasant activities, we should expect that our mood will change completely, and everything will be okay.

   True or False

6. When we experience very few activities we consider to be pleasant, we are more likely to feel depressed. Also, when we feel depressed, we don't feel like doing the kinds of activities that are likely to be a source of pleasure. **This is known as the:**

   a. Complicated bereavement

   b. Sliding depressive cycle

   c. Downward spiral of depression

   d. Resilient coping

◀ **CHAPTER FOUR** ▶

Improving Sleep

Some of the core symptoms experienced by those who have recently been in combat are sleep problems. Difficulty falling asleep or staying asleep—known as *insomnia*—is one common type of sleep problem. Additionally, people who have been deployed in combat may suffer from nightmares related to their deployment, or may wake up at night feeling terrified. Others may feel the need to stay awake to protect themselves from danger. Additionally, people may have poor sleep habits that contribute to their sleep problems, such as napping too long and too often.

Sleep problems are expected following combat deployment. Feeling on edge, sleeping for short periods of time, and nightmares all contribute to sleep problems. These problems are related to being exposed to stressful situations, and with help, should decrease over time.

In this chapter, you will learn about tools to help you sleep better. We begin, however, by reviewing last week's homework and talking more about different kinds of sleep problems that veterans may be experiencing.

■ Section A: Stages of sleep

Scientific research has shown that, when we sleep, our brain activity changes throughout the night. Electroencephalograms (EEGs) are instruments that measure the level of activity in the brain. EEGs have shown that our brains go through a series of several stages of activity as we sleep. As we enter Stage 1 of sleep, our brain activity begins to slow down. We experience a loss of awareness of time and where we are. As we enter deeper stages of sleep (especially Stages 3 to 4) we see that our brain activity becomes slower and slower. Figure 4.1, titled Sleep Stages, represents the stages our brains go through during a period of several hours of sleep. On the left are listed Stages 1 through 4. On the bottom of the graph, you will see the hours of sleep during the night, hours 1 through 8.

Wakefulness: Our brains are very active when we are awake, taking in all of the information we process.

Stage 1: During Stage 1, sleep begins. We begin to lose consciousness, body temperature, breathing, blood pressure, and pulse rates begin to decrease.

Stage 2: During Stage 2, EEG shows that our brain's activity becomes slightly slower, with bursts of rapid waves called *sleep spindles*.

Figure 4.1   Stages of sleep.

Stage 3: EEG shows that our brain's activity continues to slow during Stage 3, and brain waves becomes larger.

Stage 4: Stage 4 is the deepest stage of sleep, also consisting of still slower brain activity waves. Muscles are very relaxed and eyes are still.

Rapid Eye Movement (REM) *Sleep:* Our brain activity becomes active again during REM sleep, and our eyes move quickly back and forth under our eyelids. Our breathing, pulse, and blood pressure increase and decrease. Eighty percent of dreams and nightmares occur during REM.

The whole process of transitioning through Stages 1 to 4 takes about 90 minutes. Then we transition back up through Stages 4, 3, and 2 for several minutes, followed by a period of REM sleep. People most often have dreams and nightmares during REM sleep. This is why we remember our dreams in detail if we are awakened during REM sleep. REM lasts for only a few minutes until we cycle back into Stage 2. We cycle through these stages several times during the night.

Here are some other important details that sleep research has revealed:

■ Scientists find that depriving people of REM sleep, as opposed to other types of sleep, makes people do poorly on learning tasks. It seems that REM sleep—and perhaps dreaming—helps us to learn new material.

■ Deep sleep (Stages 3 and 4) seems to help restore the body physically. If we do not obtain the proper amount of deep sleep, then we feel tired and less rested.

■ Our bodies have a built-in daily rhythm that is affected by light, darkness, warmth, and physical activity. This is called the light/dark cycle, or the *circadian rhythm.*

This chapter can help you improve habits that will help you get a good night's sleep. But first, let's explore how poor sleep habits can mess up the sleep cycle.

■ Section B: How poor sleep habits can lead to sleep problems

- When we experience sleeplessness, a common reaction is to try to sleep more—either by napping the next day or going to bed early the next night. However, doing these things will throw the sleep cycle off.

- Alternatively, a person may drink alcohol to help him or her sleep. However, as alcohol is processed by the body, it throws off the sleep cycle even more—either causing us to wake up in the middle of the night, or simply reducing the quality of our sleep overall. Either way, the alcohol makes our sleep less restful.

- These attempts to make up for sleep work against the body's natural sleep cycle. This leads to a self-defeating cycle. The more a person tries to make up for lost sleep, the more the cycle is thrown off.

- Eventually, the person begins to become anxious about having to go to sleep. As your brain learns to associate the bed with wakefulness, anxiety, and stress, sleeping becomes an unpleasant activity (Jacobs, 1998).

- Additionally, people who have survived a highly stressful situation—such as war zone deployment—may feel hypervigilant all the time. When people are on guard, the amygdala may be over-reacting, firing up more activity in the nervous system, triggering feelings of stress or danger. This also can interfere with sleep.

- Veterans may have distressing thoughts that pop into their heads when they do not want them to. Focusing on these thoughts will also make it harder to fall asleep. The bedroom environment then becomes connected with the distressing thoughts. And when distressing thoughts are linked to the bedroom, then the bedroom itself becomes a trigger for distress.

- Nightmares and night terrors are also common in people who have gone through highly stressful events. Because nightmares can be very terrifying, after having them often, a person can start to become afraid of lying in his or her own bed or going to sleep at night. The bedroom environment then becomes linked with the fear, making it even harder to sleep.

Many of the tactics people usually resort to as an attempt to get more sleep undermine the body's natural cycle. Such tactics can lead to depression and irritability. On the other hand, good sleep habits work with the sleep cycle to restore restful sleep habits. The next section outlines good sleep habits, which we have broken down into activities taking place at nighttime, morning, and daytime. As you read the good sleep habits, think about changes you can make to your own sleep.

■ Section C: Good sleep habits

Nighttime

Activities that will help promote sleep in the evening involve slowing down physical and mental activities. Helping the body prepare for sleep include warming the body a little and relaxing the muscles. Darkness and quiet will also help tell the brain that it is time to sleep. Specific activities that are good nighttime sleep habits include:

Winding down

It is important to wind down both physically and mentally in the hour before bedtime by engaging in relaxing activities such as light reading, a calming hobby, doing relaxation exercises, or listening to relaxing music.

- During the wind-down period, avoid stimulating activities such as phone calls, arguments, work, paying bills, playing action videos, or watching TV shows.

Sleep rituals

A sleep ritual is a nightly habit or relaxing activity to help promote sleep. Sleep experts recommend that people with sleep problems spend 30 minutes to an hour prior to sleeping doing a regular activity that will ready the body and mind for sleep.

- When this activity is performed nightly for at least three weeks, it will become a habit that helps to promote sleep. Some suggestions are to:
    —Drink a warm glass of milk or decaffeinated tea.
    —Listen to relaxing music.
    —Take a warm bath or shower.
    —Read a light, and even boring book or magazine.
    —Light a candle and pray.
    —Do a simple crossword puzzle or other enjoyable puzzles.
    —Do some deep breathing or another relaxation technique to calm the body and mind.

Sleep medication

Some medications for sleep, such as Valium, are addictive and will make sleep even more difficult over time:

- Newer sleep medicines assist with strengthening the circadian rhythms, and generally do not interfere with the REM stage of sleep or one's ability to dream. Yet, there is still the possibility of physical and emotional dependence on a medicine, so they should be used with caution and only as temporary solutions.
- Antidepressants, on the other hand, can help sleep by strengthening the sleep stages and the sleep/wake cycle.
- Prescribed and over-the-counter medications should be taken as indicated by one's doctor, and should be accompanied by good sleep habits.

Bedroom environment

It is important to make your bedroom a safe, peaceful environment. Here are some suggestions of how you can do this:

- Make your bedroom comfortably dim or dark.
- Make your bed comfortable.

- Block out noises with a white noise generator, air purifier, or fan.
- Keep your bedroom temperature comfortable.
- It may help to add peaceful and comforting images to your bedroom, such as poems, prayers, or pictures of your children, pet, or a religious figure.

Keep bedroom only for sleep and sex

Your bedroom should be used for only two purposes—sleep and sex. Here are some more suggestions to help you get better sleep:

- Use the bedroom for sleep and sexual activity only.
- Do not try to go to sleep when you are not drowsy. Instead, engage in a sleep ritual until you become tired.
- If you want to go to sleep but do not fall asleep within 30 minutes, do not lie in bed tossing and turning. Instead, go to another room and engage in a quiet relaxing activity—such as reading a magazine or a boring book—until you feel drowsy.

Do not try to make up for lost sleep

Going to bed early in order to catch up on sleep seems like a good idea, but the more time you spend in bed (if you are not sleeping), the more you mess up the sleep cycle.

- Try to go to bed at the same time each night, and get up the same time each morning, even if you do not sleep well.

Some nighttime sleep habits I can change to improve my sleep include: _____

_____

_____

Morning

Activities that will improve wakefulness in the morning are those that stimulate the mind and the body. Bright lights and activity will help tell the brain that it is time to wake up. Specific good morning habits include:

Regular rising time

- Trying to catch up on lost sleep can actually hurt your ability to sleep.
- Do not sleep late after a bad night of sleep. The extra sleep in the morning will actually interfere with your sleep the following evening. Keep a regular time to get up every morning, even if you do not have to go to work.
- Instead of sleeping in late, plan an enjoyable activity in the morning such as reading the newspaper or taking a walk to help make waking up early more pleasant.

Increasing sun exposure

- One thing we can all benefit from is exposure to sunlight. Sunlight is an important timing cue for waking, and so it is helpful to be exposed to sunlight early in the day (of course, wear sunscreen as necessary).
- Even on a cloudy day, the light from the sun is much stronger than indoor lighting.
- Light from the sun improves mood and energy and will help the natural sleep cycle.

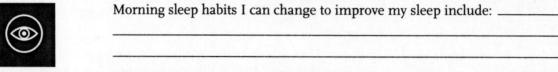

Morning sleep habits I can change to improve my sleep include: _____
_____
_____

Daytime

There are also things we can do during the day to strengthen the sleep/wake cycle.

Napping

- Taking long naps can be detrimental to you getting a good night's rest, although many cultures have naps as part of their daily routine.
- A nap as short as 10 minutes can improve mood, alertness, and mental performance. However, long naps or naps late in the day can interfere with the sleep cycle.
- Limit your nap to no more than 30 minutes and do not nap later than 4 PM.

Increasing exercise

- Not getting enough exercise can keep you from sleeping.
- Lack of physical activity can contribute to insomnia by causing a flattening of your body temperature rhythm.
- Exercise can improve sleep by causing your body temperature rhythm to rise and fall during the day.
- Exercise can also help sleep by improving your overall energy and mood.

Decreasing caffeine

- Drinking beverages containing caffeine, even if during the daytime hours can hurt your chances of getting sleep.
- Similar to alcohol and other drugs, caffeine can disrupt the sleep cycle, causing sleep to be less restful. Coffee, tea, some drinks, and chocolate all have high levels of caffeine, so they should be avoided in the afternoon and evening.

Decreasing alcohol

- It is true that drinking alcohol can help people fall asleep, however, the sleep will last for only a few hours until alcohol begins to be metabolized. Then the withdrawal from alcohol will cause mid-night awakenings or reduced sleep quality. Alcohol also tends to interfere with the REM cycle and one's ability to dream. All of these changes decrease sleep, and make it less restful.

Decreasing smoking

- If you smoke near bedtime or after waking during the night, the stimulant effect of nicotine (or withdrawal) may keep you awake—or may interfere with the sleep cycle—resulting in less restful sleep.

Decreasing stress

- Events and situations in life can cause us to have sleep problems.

- Sleep problems often begin in response to a stressful life event. It is important to perform stress-reducing activities to help you sleep better (see Chapter 2).

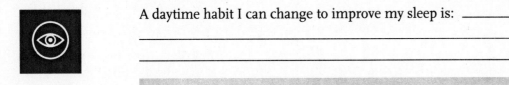

A daytime habit I can change to improve my sleep is: _____

_____

_____

■ Section D: Nightmares and night terrors

After being in-country, veterans may experience at least a few nightmares or night terrors:

- During *night terrors,* people wake up terrified but cannot remember a dream.

- During *nightmares,* people may feel as though they are reliving the event, or may feel the same fear, helplessness, or rage that may have been experienced during their war experience.

- Night terrors and nightmares are not a sign that you are going crazy. Rather, they are your mind's way of processing a stressful experience.

- Some veterans try to avoid nightmares, by using drugs or alcohol, or by avoiding sleep altogether.

- These attempted solutions only lead to new problems, such as substance dependence and sleep deprivation. This also usually results in more irritability and depression, poorer memory, and increased stress and anxiety.

Coping strategies for nightmares and night terrors

We suggest the following for coping with nightmares or night terrors:

- If you are confused or anxious after waking from a nightmare or night terror, it is helpful to "ground" yourself by shifting your focus to the room around you. Look around (if there is enough light to see) and begin labeling the objects you see in the room. For example, say to yourself or out loud "That is my desk. Those are my clothes. This is my bed. I am in my room. That is my partner next to me." until you are less confused.

- It is helpful to get up and go to another room to get your bearings. If you still feel confused or anxious, "ground" yourself by focusing on and labeling the objects in that room. It may take a while to reorient yourself to where you are and the present time.

- It is helpful to write the nightmare down. Doing this can make the dream less real and help you calm down faster. It can also be a good way to begin to share the dream with someone close to you, which can help you begin to have control over the nightmare.

- After you feel reoriented to the present, practice your sleep ritual.

- If possible, reach out to someone you feel safe with—who supports you. If you live with others, find time to talk to them about the fact that you are having nightmares. Discuss ways in which you both might want to handle the situation.

- A small percentage of sufferers act out their nightmares in their sleep. You may want to rearrange your bedroom so that you are safe. If you share your bed with a partner, you may need to make sure he or she is not in harm's way.

- If your nightmares do not decrease over time, know that there are effective treatments available (Davis & Wright, 2007; Krystal & Davidson, 2007).

■ Section E: Treatment for sleep problems

There are effective treatments for sleep problems. However, choosing the one that is right for you will depend upon your situation. If your sleep problems do not go away with time, contact a mental health provider who has expertise in sleep disorders and PTSD. Therapy that addresses the way you think and act (called cognitive behavioral therapy) can help bring about long-term relief of sleep problems. Cognitive behavioral therapy for sleep disorders targets your beliefs and behaviors that can make sleep problems worse. Specific therapy and medications for nightmares can also be very helpful in improving sleep and other stress reactions. Breathing and relaxation therapies also may be used to help reduce muscle tension and promote sleep.

Additionally, many anti-depressants can help improve sleep and strengthen the sleep/wake cycle and sleep stages. For example, antidepressants such as Wellbutrin, Prozac, Paxil, and Celexa may actually help restore the natural sleep cycle. Of course, sleep medications are available for quick, short-term relief of insomnia and nightmares. But some sleep medications can be addictive and may have side effects, so check with your doctor to find out which treatment is best for you.

▶ When to talk to your doctor

Have you or someone you know been:

- Having difficulty falling or staying asleep several times a week?
- Having repeated nightmares or night terrors?

- Repeatedly waking up screaming, crying, or feeling panicked, but not knowing why?
- Feeling so overwhelmed that you might hurt yourself or someone else?

Did you respond YES to ONE or more of these questions? If so, talk to your doctor right away.

▶ **The heart of the matter**

Some of the core symptoms experienced by those who have returned from war are sleep problems—such as insomnia and nightmares. Additionally, individuals often have poor sleep habits that contribute to their sleep problems, such as napping too frequently or too long, or keeping an irregular sleep schedule. Some veterans suffering from post-deployment reactions may also try to fix their problem with "solutions" that only make the problem worse (e.g., using alcohol or other drugs, or by sleeping all day). Good sleep habits involve working with the body's natural sleep cycles so you can sleep better.

- Please turn to the end of the chapter and take the quiz. Remember that the quizzes are a good way to review some of the important points in the chapter.
- Please note that helpful resources and references on insomnia are provided for you in the reference section at the back of this book.
- Please take a few minutes to complete the brief quiz at the end of this chapter. It will help you remember what you have learned in this chapter.

▶ **On your own**

1. Complete the Phone Calling Exercise Worksheet, in the same way that you did for the last session. Remember to note your SUDS before and after each call.

2. Identify three new sleep habits you are willing to try every day for the next three weeks:

   1. _____

   2. _____

   3. _____

3. Use the Sleep Habit Schedule on page 51 to write down the days and times that you plan to practice your new sleep habits. You may want to schedule more. Perhaps you may want to choose one type of activity from each category for each day.

Phone Calling Exercise Worksheet

Name: _____

Session Number: _____

Question: _____

Person Called	Date	Your Own SUDS Before (0–10)	Answer/Topic	Call Length	Your Own SUDS After (0–10)

Sleep Habits Schedule

Use this schedule to write down the days and times that you plan to practice your new sleep habits. Keep the schedule somewhere where you will see it daily.

	Monday	Tuesday	Wednesday	Thursday	Friday	Saturday	Sunday
0600 hrs.							
0700 hrs.							
0800 hrs.							
0900 hrs.							
1000 hrs.							
1100 hrs.							
1200 hrs.							
1300 hrs.							
1400 hrs.							
1500 hrs.							
1600 hrs.							
1700 hrs.							
1800 hrs.							
1900 hrs.							
2000 hrs.							
2100 hrs.							
2200 hrs.							
Night ↓							

STRATEGIES FOR MANAGING STRESS AFTER WAR

Name: _____

Date: _____ _____ / _____ _____ / _____ _____

1. We have dreams every night that we sleep.
   True or False

2. Sleeping in late is a good way to catch up on lost sleep.
   True or False

3. Alcohol and certain medications (such as Valium, Xanax, and over-the-counter sleep medications) can mess up our sleep cycle.
   True or False

4. Antidepressants can mess up our sleep cycle.
   True or False

5. Taking a 60-minute nap can mess up the sleep cycle.
   True or False

6. If you cannot fall asleep at night, it is best to perform a stressful, highly demanding task that will tire you out and help you fall asleep.
   True or False

7. If you wake up and cannot get back to sleep, it is best to get out of bed (even in the middle of the night) and engage in a light, somewhat boring, activity.
   True or False

8. One way to cope with a nightmare is to write it down.
   True or False

CHAPTER FIVE

Dealing with Anger

People returning from long deployments often feel irritable and angry. Because some veterans may feel on edge, they are at risk for getting into trouble—be it with their spouse or partner, coworkers, supervisors, strangers, or the law. To prevent problems associated with high irritability and anger, it is important to become aware of cues that can let you know when you when these feelings are increasing. The purpose of this chapter is to raise awareness of your irritability and anger so that you are better able to identify them and prevent problems from taking place. We also discuss how anger can be channeled in either healthy or unhealthy ways. We conclude the chapter with a basic technique to help you reduce the chance that your anger will get you in trouble.

■ Section A: What is anger?

Anger is a feeling we have when the world is not going the way we want. What happens to the body when a person becomes angry?

- Muscles become contracted and tense
- Heart pumps faster
- Breathing becomes quicker
- Stomach tightens
- Body feels hot

When we get angry, adrenaline and other chemicals pour into the bloodstream to shift the body into high gear, generating energy for action.

What happens mentally when we get angry?

When we become very angry, it really interferes with our thinking. When adrenaline and other chemicals in the body become overly charged, the logical part of the brain gets tuned off, and our behavior becomes more impulsive, illogical, and desperate. The angrier we are, the more foolish we get.

What are some feelings, sensations, or thoughts *you* have when you get angry? ____

_____

_____

■ Section B: Risks and benefits from anger

How can anger be hurtful?

Anger can lead to a slew of problems, such as:

- Poor thinking and decision making
- Ruined relationships
- Divorce
- Work problems
- Lost promotions
- Dismissal from jobs
- Arguments or fights
- Spousal abuse
- Legal and financial problems
- Incarceration
- Health problems (e.g., headaches, heart disease, high cholesterol, immune system disorders, chronic pain, stomach disorders, diarrhea, and early death)

Should we try to stop feeling angry?

No! As long as we are alive we will have reasons to be angry from time to time. Some levels of anger and conflict are inescapable in relationships. Therefore, we need to learn resilient ways to cope with anger, and to keep it from being too frequent or too intense.

What is healthy anger?

Anger that is expressed in helpful ways is healthy anger. When we are able to react to situations with logic, we can be angry without letting the feeling get us in trouble. Additionally, we can channel the energy we get from anger in healthy ways to help motivate ourselves, and help us achieve what we want.

How can anger help us?

- Anger can help people reach their goals.
- Anger can give people energy.
- Anger can motivate people to work harder.
- Anger can help people solve problems.
- Anger can help people handle emergencies.

List some healthy ways that you can channel your anger: _____
_____
_____
_____

■ Section C: How can I prevent harmful anger?

It is very important to take some time to step back from a situation that is triggering feelings of anger. It is important to be able to think logically so that you identify a healthy way to handle the feeling.

There are three important steps to prevent harmful anger:

1. Notice when your stress or anger level is increasing.

2. Build in a pause or take a time-out.

3. Identify healthy ways to resolve ager.

Step 1: Monitoring signs of anger and stress

The first step is to pay attention to your level of anger, just as it is important to get a feel for the level of stress you may be experiencing. An anger scale, similar to the SUDS stress rating scale, can be a helpful guide in this respect (see Figure 5.1).

■ As discussed in a previous section, it is important to keep your stress level below 5. Similarly, when anger rises above 5, it is a cue to use relaxation methods or some other healthy coping behavior to restore your ability to think. Remember that when your level of irritation and anger are already high—when you are "running hot"— even something small can bump you up higher to where you are more likely to react badly. Keeping your overall level of irritation lower and noticing your anger climbing earlier gives you more time to catch it when your anger starts getting higher.

■ Practice tuning in to your own cues that help you to know when you are getting angry. Remember that these cues might be:

—Changes in your body, such as "butterflies" or tension in your stomach, beginning to sweat, feeling your heartbeat get faster, tension in your arms or chest, etc.

—Other sensations in your body, such as feeling dizzy or lightheaded, a headache, or nausea.

—Specific repetitive thoughts, such as "I can't believe we're having this same argument *again*—every week it's the same thing," "they're doing this on purpose to make me mad," or "I'll teach them not to mess with me," or things that we tell ourselves when we are getting upset (and which also make us *more* upset).

What are some cues that tell you when you are becoming angry? _____

_____

Where is your anger level right now? _____ / 10

Figure 5.1   Anger scale.

Step 2: Build in a pause or take a time-out

Once people understand how to monitor their anger, they can take additional steps to stop themselves from acting out in ways that could harm themselves or others. When they find themselves in a situation where they are feeling very angry, they must resist acting impulsively—instead they can distract themselves or remove themselves from the situation so that they can calm down. It is important to calm down and think clearly before acting.

The easiest way to calm down is to build a pause in between the feeling of anger and your reaction to it—this is commonly referred to as a time-out (Edleson & Tolman, 1992; Paymar, 1993; Pence & Paymar, 1993; Rosenbaum & Leisring, 2001). Some people are able to calm down by counting to ten. Some people can think of a person who is calming to them, a particular scene (such as a lake), or some other relaxing image (such as the color blue) that will distract them from the issue that is getting them riled. It is important to practice and find the time-out method that works best for you.

What is a time-out?

A time-out is a technique for people who sometimes get into trouble because of acting impulsively, or who react too quickly or too extremely because of anger. The purpose of the time-out is to provide you with an opportunity to step back from the situation that is making you angry. Stepping back, and temporarily removing yourself from the situation, gives you time to cool off, think about things, and make better choices. Time-outs are described more at the end of this chapter (see the handout on pages 58–59 of this chapter called Time-out).

If you are in a long-term relationship and have problems with anger, we suggest talking about time-outs with your spouse or partner. Have a preplanned signal that lets your spouse or partner know that the situation is getting out of hand and a cool-down period is needed. For instance, in one couple either party would hold up their hand in a halt posture, and say "I am taking a time-out." The other party would then step back and allow their spouse or partner an hour to cool down. It is important to plan for these situations ahead of time to make the time-out effective.

Here are some important questions to think about and answer for yourself:

- Who can I use time-outs with?
- What are some situations that a time-out can help with?
- When do I know that I need to use a time-out? What are the cues to look for that tell me I am becoming angry—physically, emotionally, or otherwise?
- What can I use as my preplanned signals?
- Where can I go during a time-out to cool off?
- What are some ways that I can calm down when I am becoming very angry?

Step 3: Identify healthy ways to resolve anger

Once you cool down, you can think about healthy ways to deal with your feelings. When you are calmer, it is easier to explore your options so you can better understand the actual cause of the anger, and make a logical decision about what you are going to do.

The cause of the anger may or may not be obvious. For example, you may be yelling at your spouse or partner for burning dinner, but you are really angry with a coworker for snubbing you earlier in the day. You may want to explode at someone in line at the store, but really you know you are irritated because you slept poorly the night before.

If there is a conflict that you are angry about, you can then take positive steps to resolve the problem, rather than letting the angry feelings linger. It often is important to talk to others (for example a friend, family member, therapist, or pastor) who are not part of the conflict, about your problem.

What are some healthy things that *you* can do to help resolve your anger? _____

_____

_____

■ Section D: Treatments for anger

If you have noticed your anger level has been peaking a lot lately, and have a hard time controlling it, please know there is help. One very important part of treatments for anger is in helping a person to identify the specific cues that relate to their anger. There are anger management workshops people can take to learn more about managing anger reactions and practice more ways of calming down. There are also medications that can be helpful for people who are raging a lot of the time and have trouble controlling their anger.

▶ When to talk to your doctor

Have you or someone you know been:

- Making poor decisions that have been hurting you or someone you care about?
- Having a lot of conflicts with your boss, supervisor, or coworkers? Or are you having legal problems or trouble holding a job?
- Having trouble communicating with and getting along with your spouse or significant other?
- Feeling so overwhelmed that you might hurt yourself or someone else?

Did you answer YES to ONE or more of these questions? If so, talk to your doctor right away.

▶ The heart of the matter

A lot of veterans report feeling on edge, easily frustrated, and quick to anger. You may have just returned from months on end during which you sacrificed your own well-being for this nation's safety, or you may have been back for some time. You may have had to adhere to strict limits to what you could do to protect yourself. You may feel responsible or angry for things that were not in your control. Please remember that it will take time to transition from the war zone, and that it also takes skilled practice and effort to help our system adjust to being back. The high level of energy that you may have used to keep yourself alive is no longer needed, but it will take awhile for your body to learn that. In the meantime, it is important to take extra steps so that you do not do something you regret. When you channel your anger in healthy ways, you can use anger to achieve what you want.

■ Please turn to the end of the chapter and take the quiz. Remember that the quizzes are a good way to review some of the important points in the chapter.

▶ On your own

1. Complete the Phone Calling Exercise. Remember to note your SUDS before and after each call. Complete details about this exercise are included in the On Your Own section at the end of Chapter 1.

2. Identify a possible future situation where you may have to deal with your anger:
   ■ What are the cues to look for—physically, emotionally, or otherwise—that will let you know that you are becoming angry?
   ■ What are some healthy things that you can do to help resolve the situation?

3. Practice using the time-out technique. Plan ahead, by thinking about the type of situations in which you might need a time-out, and how you will implement it.

▶ Time-out

This is a useful technique for people who have trouble managing anger productively, and instead sometimes react to anger by acting out in unhealthy ways.* The purpose of a time-out is to provide you with an opportunity to step back from the situation that is making you angry and to think about your options before you make a decision about what you are going to do. In order to be successful, you must practice this technique consistently. If you have a partner, review these guidelines with him or her, so that you can agree on how to use the time-out technique, and so that each of you will know what to expect.

1. *Monitor:* When you are having an argument, or in other situations that you anticipate may be upsetting to you, closely monitor your SUDS and your level of anger.

---

* Adapted from Edleson & Tolman, 1992; Paymar, 1993; Pence & Paymar, 1993.

2. *Notify:* When you notice yourself getting angry to a such a level that you think you may act in a dangerous or hurtful way, say out loud to yourself and the person with whom you are angry: "I'm beginning to feel really angry, and I need to take a time-out."

3. *Explain:* Tell the other person where you are going, and when you will return. Usually one hour is a reasonable amount of time—enough to cool down, but not so much that you are simply avoiding the issues.

4. *Positive action:* During the time-out, choose a positive place and activity to help calm yourself down, and begin improving the situation. During this time do *not* use alcohol or drugs, and avoid driving. It is best to do something healthy that will help you to get your anger out, such as going for a walk, exercising, doing a noncompetitive and nonviolent hobby or sport, or talking to a "positive" person who can help you to calm down. This can be a great time to call someone else in the group for support. You may also use relaxation skills, such as muscle relaxation, deep breathing, and relaxing imagery. During this time, take a "mental" time-out and don't allow your thoughts to escalate your anger.

5. *Coming back:* Return on time, based on the amount of time you said you would be away. Call your partner if you are coming back earlier or later than you said, so that they also have had enough time to cool down, are not surprised, or waiting for you.

6. *Offer to talk:* When you return, ask the other person if he or she would like to talk with you. If you both want to discuss the situation, tell the other person why you think you became angry. You may also want to talk about what it was like for you to take a time-out. If you feel yourself again wanting to explode, take another time-out.

7. *Respect his or her desires:* If the other person does not want to talk, do not force it. Respect the other person's need not to discuss it at this time. Some topics of conversation are too "charged" to talk about right away or without a helper. Put the issue on the shelf for a while, accepting that it is too difficult for the two of you to discuss it alone. Even if it is an important issue, *remember that your first priority is to prevent violence.*

Time-outs can be hard to do. Why? Because some of us are taught to believe that only a coward will walk away from a fight. Your impulse will be to stay and finish it, or at least to get in the last word. You may feel your self-respect is on the line. Even worse, you may feel very afraid when you walk away. Consider these "hot thoughts" as your enemies, not your protectors. Remember, an argument does *not* mean that your life is in danger, and in a relationship violence will *not* get you what you want. Practicing this new skill is part of stopping the cycle of destructiveness, anger, and depression, and taking a step toward more effective coping.

Finally, like learning any new skill, taking a time-out may be difficult at first. Many people tend to give up quickly after initial failure. Remember, you have to unlearn many years of destructive behavior and learn something new. It will not happen quickly. It will not happen perfectly the first time, or even the second. However, with conscious commitment and practice, taking time-outs will become easier in time.

Phone Calling Exercise Worksheet

Name: _____

Session Number: _____

Question: _____

Person Called	Date	Your Own SUDS Before (0–10)	Answer/Topic	Call Length	Your Own SUDS After (0–10)

Name: _____

Date: _____ _____ / _____ _____ / _____ _____

1. Being angry for long periods of time may lead to:
   a. High blood pressure
   b. Early death
   c. Stomach disorders
   d. All of the above

2. Which of the following is an **unhelpful** thing to do when you get very angry?
   a. Count to 10
   b. Take a time out
   c. Try to argue your point
   d. All of the above

3. Which of the following is a **helpful** use of your anger?
   a. Use anger to help you work harder
   b. Use anger to help motivate you to reach a goal
   c. Use anger to help you solve a problem
   d. All of the above

4. If your anger level is 5 or over (on a scale from 1 to 10) you should perform a healthy coping behavior.
   True or False

5. Veterans coming home from the war zone tend to be very calm and relaxed.
   True or False

6. Anger is a "bad" emotion that can only lead to conflict and aggression.
   True or False

7. List three cues that tell people when they are becoming angry:

   _____

   _____

   _____

CHAPTER SIX

Reintegrating with Society

You may be having some really mixed feelings about your time at war and about your return to the United States. Maybe you thought that the transition would be easy, but you are finding out that is not completely true. In this session, we discuss common difficulties that many veterans face as they adjust back to civilian life.

► Reintegration

Going from the foxhole to your front porch is a profound change to make in a short amount of time. Sometimes you may feel like you are still fighting the war. It takes time to adapt back to civilian life, and you may still find yourself acting in ways you never have before. When you get in tighter spaces or crowds, you may feel trapped or in danger. You may still feel on guard, even at times when logic says that things really are safe. It is possible that you may be overwhelmed by noise and confusion, even in your home. You could be on a totally different schedule for sleeping and eating than your family.

What are your biggest concerns as you transition back into civilian society? _____

_____

_____

■ Section A: Major reintegration issue—Control

Going through really difficult and painful experiences during war deployments can leave people with a feeling of being out of control. Many people feel like they cannot control what is going on in their environment or in their lives. In fact, there are many things in our lives that we simply do *not* have the power to control. For example, you may not have control over parts of your life because you are in the military. Here are some examples of things you may not have control over:

- Where you are stationed
- When you will be deployed
- How long you stay on deployment
- How other people behave
- Crowds at a grocery store
- The weather
- Unwanted memories and other combat stress reactions

What types of things do you feel you do not have control over right now?

_____

_____

_____

However, there are plenty of things in life we *can* control. For example:

- We *can* control what we do in our free time.
- We *can* control who we spend our time with.
- We *can* control how we treat other people.
- We *can* control out attitudes about life.
- We *can* control our choices about our future.

Name some things that you *do* have control over right now.

_____

_____

_____

It is important to recognize the things in life that we *can* control and those things that are *not* in our control. When we put our focus and efforts on things within our control, we are able to be more effective and more successful.

■ Section B: Major reintegration issue—Hypervigilance

Vigilant people are alert to danger in the environment. In a war zone, maintaining a high level of vigilance is extremely useful. Being on constant alert for danger is critical in keeping yourself alive because you never know which person or what item might be deadly on the street. In the war zone, staying highly alert becomes second nature.

Over time, however, people in a war zone often get used to feeling threatened—in their environment or with other people—and they may continue to feel that way when they return home. When people return from war, it is common for them to be *hypervigilant,* overly alert for possible dangers. They may be hypervigilant because they overestimate the possibility of danger.

Hypervigilance is not useful in a safe environment. In fact, as we discussed in earlier chapters, long-term hypervigilance can be dangerous—it interferes with sleep, contributes to excess levels of stress and anger, and actually makes people *less* likely to detect real danger, and less capable of dealing with actual dangerous situations.

It is possible that you have been overestimating danger as well. Your friends or family members may make comments that you look tense, or you may be avoiding activities that you used to enjoy. These feelings are expected for those returning from war. It may take time to adjust to being with other people or in unknown environments.

There are a number of ways that you can overcome hypervigilance. Initially, your body and brain have to be retrained to accept that many situations may feel uncomfortable, even when they are not dangerous. For example, you may feel uncomfortable being around lots of people—such as being in a crowd or going to the mall. To begin getting used to doing some of the things you enjoyed in the past, gradually practice being around other people. You may want to start with small groups. Also, starting off in places you are familiar with will help you adjust back to the fact that you are no longer in danger.

When you begin spending more time in environments that might trigger reminders of the war zone, remember to monitor to your stress cues and SUDS, and use your tools—belly breathing, progressive muscle relaxation, grounding—as you practice tolerating the environment. With practice, you can slowly recondition yourself to feel comfortable in situations you used to enjoy—and even begin to enjoy them again.

Some tools that I can use to cope with hypervigilance include:

_____

_____

_____

■ Section C: Major reintegration issue—Coping with civilians

Expect a culture shock for a while as you adjust back to life in the United States. You have spent time in a foreign country, perhaps in a battle zone among the enemy and routinely facing possible death or injury. After returning from the war zone, everyday life can seem boring. It may feel like not being at war is betraying the friends you left behind. You may feel angry because civilians are not paying attention to what the military is doing. You will run into people who have strong opinions about the war. Some are okay with it—and some are not. And some will ask very stupid and insensitive questions.

A good way to deal with the return to civilian life is to think about the types of problems you might run into, and how you might deal with them. Thinking ahead about common problems veterans face, and how you might handle them, can head off problems before they begin.

As an example, you may want to think ahead about healthy ways to handle people who provoke you. Consider the following:

■ What would you do if someone made an offensive statement to you? How would you handle it if it were different people?

—A friend

—Someone you work with

—Close family member

—A stranger

▶ Hold on! Did you need a time-out?

In the anger chapter, we talked about time-outs. To repeat, time-outs are great because they defuse the situation. It's like breaking up two boxers and putting them back in their own corners of the boxing ring. It gives people a few minutes to think about things, to sort things out. After returning from the war zone, it may be harder to keep your cool and it may take extra time to chill out.

■ You may want to go back to the anger section and review what you learned about healthy ways to manage and reduce anger.

Reintegration plan exercise

We cannot change other people or past events. But when we examine ourselves, we find that we do have control over many of the choices in our lives. It is extremely important for us to recognize when we *do* and *do not* have control, so that we can take care of ourselves. It is important for you to be able to answer these questions:

■ What things or people trigger my anger or stress reactions? What sets me off?

■ How do I deal with anger or other feelings when I am triggered?

■ Are the ways I am dealing with this bad for me? If so, what can I start doing differently? (be specific)

■ Section D: Treatments for reintegration difficulties

We have talked about how there are a lot of different areas in your life that have changed since you got back home. An area that requires adjusting is being able to deal with hypervigilance and hyperarousal. Another is getting used to crowds. It might be difficult and challenging to talk with civilians now. Other people may not understand what is going on, or may not care. If any of these continue to be difficult for you, please know there is help available.

Treatments for reintegration stress will vary depending on what your main concerns are now. But no one needs to suffer alone. Treatments and counselors are available to help you through this time.

▶ When to talk to your doctor

Have you or someone you know been:

■ Feeling trapped, suffocated, closed in, or panicky when you are in tight-spaced areas or in crowds?

■ Feeling angry at or disconnected from others, or like no one can understand what you are going through?

- Feeling overwhelmed by your reactions?
- Thinking you might hurt yourself or someone else?

Did you answer YES to ONE or more of these questions? If so, talk to your doctor right away.

▶ The heart of the matter

In this chapter, you learned that the reactions that you may be having right now are common for service members who have come back from a war. This is an adjustment process for you. As a warrior, you have so much strength and courage inside of you. If you doubt this for even a second, please remember you did what most people never do—you survived deployment! You survived then, and you have what it takes to keep on surviving.

- Please turn to the end of the chapter and take the quiz. Remember that the quizzes are a good way to review some of the important points in the chapter.

▶ On your own

1. Complete the Phone Calling Exercise. Remember to note your SUDS before and after each call. Complete details about this exercise are included in the On Your Own section at the end of Chapter 1.

2. Do the Reintegration Plan exercise in this chapter to plan what you will do to cope with people who trigger anger or stress. Continue to practice good communication and time-out skills with others. Keep using your new skills, and you will find that things go more smoothly when there are problems.

Phone Calling Exercise Worksheet

Name: _____

Session Number: _____

Question: _____

Person Called	Date	Your Own SUDS Before (0–10)	Answer/Topic	Call Length	Your Own SUDS After (0–10)

Name: _____

Date: _____ _____ / _____ _____ / _____ _____

1. People who are hypervigilant:
   a. Always help other people who are in need
   b. Think they are sick even when they are well.
   c. Are overly alert for danger even when danger is not present.
   d. All of the above.

2. We can control every aspect of our environment and our life.
   True or False

3. "Thinking ahead" is an important part of making healthy decisions and reintegrating with society.
   True or False

4. What are some situations or people that trigger stress reactions for you?

   _____

   _____

   _____

5. What healthy coping behaviors can I use to deal with the people and/or situations that trigger stress reactions?

   _____

   _____

   _____

Reintegrating with Family and Friends

When warriors return from deployment, the number one thing they talk about is how they now feel different. It is true! You have changed and you are different. And those around you have changed, too. Time changes everyone. Maybe you feel happy to be back in the United States, or maybe you do not. Often warriors have grown used to being in the war zone and wish they were back there. You may be dealing with practical problems. For example, you may be returning to family problems that you had before you left, and are not feeling happy about having to deal with them again. In this chapter, we describe strategies that can help you deal with these problems so you can reintegrate back with your family and friends.

▶ The important role of families and friends

Often, the primary source of support for the veteran is his or her spouse or partner, parents, grandparents, children, siblings, and other extended family members or close friends. For many war veterans over the years, family and friends have been extremely important in helping them deal with and overcome transition stress. This is because families and friendships provide:

- Companionship
- A sense of belonging
- Self-esteem that can help prevent depression and guilt
- Opportunities to make a positive contribution by helping others
- Practical support
- Emotional support to help in coping with life stressors

Families and friends play an important role in helping you connect with other people. If you are having a rough time re-connecting with those you used to be close with, you may be feeling very frustrated. You may also be wondering if things will ever get back to normal.

■ Section A: Connecting with your family and friends

Not everyone is able to make the transition back to family life with ease. You have changed. Your family and friends have changed as well while you were gone. It is possible that you have wondered if you still fit into your family. It will take time for everyone to get used to each other again. You may be feeling different and even acting different. Because of this, your behavior can affect others in your life.

Below are some changes that other veterans have experienced. Have you noticed any of these in your own life?

- Some veterans have felt a loss of interest in activities. This can confuse family and friends and make them feel cut off or left out.

- Some veterans have difficulty trusting and feeling close to others. As a result, family and friends may feel hurt and betrayed.

- Some veterans may feel like they need to be in control at all times and not show emotions besides anger, which can hurt their relationships.

- Some veterans may be reluctant to talk about what happened in the war zone, which might make family or friends feel left out or insignificant.

How are the problems you are having right now affecting those close to you?

■ Section B: Special issues for couples and children

Veterans often report changes in their relationships with their spouse or partner following deployment. Problems commonly come up that can make getting back together as a couple very challenging and difficult.

Here are some typical problems that you may face as you transition back to being a couple:

- Face-to-face communication may be hard.

- Sexual closeness may be awkward, or it may be difficult to connect like you used to.

- Because of stress you may have lost interest in sexual activities, which may lead to your spouse or partner feeling hurt.

- You may feel closer to your military buddies, and feel like your spouse or partner is a stranger.

- The roles you all used to play for basic household chores may have changed.

- Your spouse or partner may be more independent now, or he or she may have learned new coping skills.

- You may have changed in your outlook and priorities in life. Or, maybe your spouse or partner's priorities have changed while you were away.

Similarly, returning parents sometimes face common problems related to their children. Here are some typical problems that you may face as you transition back to being a parent:

- Your children have grown and may be different in many ways.

- Your children may not remember you, or may be slow to hug you or communicate with you.

- If you have younger children, they can sometimes become clingy or act younger than their age because of the adjustment.
- If you have older children, it is possible that they may be acting indifferent, as if they do not care about you.

Are any of these true of your experience? What problems are you having with your spouse, partner, or children right now?

It is a very common for veterans and their significant others to believe that once they return to the United States they will transition back into home and society life easily and that the change will be a smooth one. Unfortunately, this is sometimes far from the case.

Please know that it is expected for your family life to be affected after coming back from war. You may wonder if it can ever be okay again. A lot of veterans think they should be happy all of the time because they are back with their families, and they feel guilty that they do not feel that way. Maybe you feel that way, too. We have found that there are some rules of thumb that can help people readjust to family life again. We will discuss these in the next section.

■ Section C: Suggestions for reintegration

Here are some suggestions to help you transition back with your family and friends:

- Take time to listen to your spouse or partner, children, and other important family members and friends. Make individual time for each person.
- Take time, such as a whole day away, for just you and your spouse or partner to renew your relationship.
- Go slowly when reestablishing your place in the family. Roles may have changed and will need to be renegotiated.
- You might need to take some breaks by yourself or with your buddies, for yourself. Or, your spouse or partner may need some breaks at times because he or she is not used to having you there all of the time. It will be an adjustment for both of you, as well as your children.
- Make efforts to explain to your family and friends what you are feeling and what you would like or need from them. It is very helpful to communicate any changes to your family so that they understand why you may be different. Remember that family members may need help understanding how you have changed.
- Keep in mind that your experience was and *is* very different from that of your family. Be patient and remember that it will take some time for all of you to readjust back to "normal life."
- Share with your family some stories about your deployment. You do not have to share everything—just what feels comfortable for both you and your listener. This can provide you with some more emotional support, and help your family to know that they are important enough that you feel comfortable in sharing a part

of you with them. It can help all of you heal and bridge the gap that formed while you were away.

- Support and reinforce good things your family has done while you were gone.
- Be prepared to make some adjustments. A family is not a military unit. You may have to renegotiate with them regarding family responsibilities and routines.

Returning home is difficult to do when things are not going as planned. It may be important to cut yourself and your family some slack. Remember that it takes time to get used to being back—be patient with yourself and your family. You all need to get used to each other, as you currently are.

■ Section D: Dealing with the change

So, the question that you may be asking yourself is: My problems are much bigger than this, what do I do to make it better? Well, first off, we cannot control everything that happens outside of ourselves. What's more important is *how we control ourselves.*

You *do* have control over how you deal with all of this! And that is *very* important to remember.

Communicating with others, maybe slowly at first, will help to solve these problems. But every one of us needs support from people in our lives. Bucking up and playing it strong all the time will only make it harder for you and your family to heal. Other people can give you perspective and ideas about how to tackle a problem. If opening up to your friends and family is difficult for you now, here are three steps to help guide you:

1. First, remember that it is common to be having difficulties and a lot of mixed emotions right now. It is expected to feel frustrated at times. Solving problems with others will involve balancing other people's needs with your own.

2. Second, remember that healthy relationships are associated with lower levels of depression. Examples of healthy relationships are those in which a person feels:
    - Liked,
    - Respected,
    - Understood,
    - Appreciated, and
    - Accepted (Lewinsohn, Hoberman, Teri, & Hautziner, 1985).

Identify people in your life who make you feel like this. These people are those you feel comfortable talking with and who are probably better able to help you.

In the following space, list people you would feel okay talking with or asking for help when you need it. This can be your friends, family members, people from your phone calling exercise, coworkers, boss, chaplain, or a therapist. Try to think of people from different areas of your life (e.g., not all service members, or not all family members). If you do not have people in your life who you feel respect and accept you, think about others—chaplains, therapists, or other professionals who can listen to you. If you have more than five people, great. This is just a start:

1. _____

2. _____

3. _____

4. _____

5. _____

3. Last, actually *talk* with people you feel comfortable with about the problems you are having. Identify at least one person from the previous list who you will talk to about problems reintegrating in the week ahead.

■ Section E: Fighting fair

What if talking with others is not working? What if you are having a problem with a friend or family member? What if you are very angry? One of the things that can make it hardest to talk to people close to us—like a spouse or romantic partner—is arguments. When disagreements come up it is important to be able to resolve issues. In other words, it is important to "strike while the iron is hot." This means, do not stuff your feelings in or expect your family and friends to know what is bothering you. Express your feelings when you are upset in a calm and civilized manner. Bottling in your resentment will only create further tension, which will lead to resentment and dysfunction in your relationships.

Some people believe that arguing in a relationship is harmful. In fact, all relationships require two people to be able to disagree, and to be able to figure out how to get through it together. However, it is also important to be able to discuss problems in a way that *builds up* the relationship, instead of breaking it down. A number of experts have discussed helpful ways of improving communication and building better relationships (Beck, 1988; Gottman & Silver, 1999; Guerney, 1977; Jacobson & Christensen, 1996). Following the advice of these experts, we can learn how to discuss, and even argue, in a way that helps instead of hurts. We can learn how to *fight fair*! Here are some rules for fighting fair:

Rules for fighting fair

Plan ahead

Rather than waiting for an argument to start with someone, schedule time to discuss a problem. Let the person know that you want to work toward a solution during this time, and agree on a time to talk about it. This will give both of you time to think about the important issue, and to approach the discussion calmly, with no surprises. Choose a time when you can talk without interruptions and distractions to bring up problems before they get too big.

Keep your eyes on the prize

In an argument, if the goal is to "win at any cost," then the relationship will suffer. However, if we want things to go better in the relationship, then we need to focus on a different goal—reaching a resolution that is peaceful and satisfying for both of us.

Focus on yourself by using "I" statements

When you bring up an issue, talk about yourself by starting off with the word "I." Tell the other person how you feel, and what you think about the issue. Making accusations is not going to help resolve the problem. When we start using "you" statements (such as "You make me angry" or "You never help me" or "You always . . .") the other person is likely to feel blamed and become defensive. Instead, it is better to start off with "I" by making statements such as, "*I feel* angry when you turn the TV sound up high" or "*I feel* frustrated when you let the kids fight with each other."

Stick to one topic

Bring up a *specific* issue that has recently occurred. Tell the other person exactly what happened, and why it bothered you. Avoid using the words "always" or "all the time." For example, instead of saying "You nag me all the time!" say "I feel angry when you tell me not to watch TV, because I need a break sometimes."

Resist the urge to bring up other topics or other past incidents. Do not make the discussion a time to list everything the other person has ever done wrong. Keep focused on resolving the specific issue at hand.

Stay calm

When we become too "jacked up" and upset, we are not likely to think clearly, and we are more likely to say and do things that just will not help the situation. You have learned a lot of skills you can use to help yourself to stay calm—put them into practice here. It may be important to take breaks during the discussion, so that you and your partner can use skills to stay calm. Use these breaks as a way to calm down—not to make yourself angrier, or to keep thinking about what you want to say next. This will also make it more likely that you can continue to use all of these rules for fighting fair.

No "below the belt" shots

Name-calling, foul language, threats, and sarcasm will make arguments worse. Each of these distracts from the main point. They will destroy an argument, rather than helping to find common ground, and can destroy a relationship. A common saying from recovery programs puts it this way: "Say what you mean, mean what you say, but don't say it mean."

If you are having a hard time thinking of what to say to your family or friends, use the Communication Plan Exercise to help you get prepared.

■ Section F: Communication plan exercise

There are four basic steps in communicating: (1) identify the problem, (2) decide what you want or need, (3) state the message, and (4) get feedback from the person. You need all four steps to have a two-way conversation. Practice these skills again and again to better deal with problems in your relationships with people:

1. *Identify the problem* that you want to resolve with a friend or someone you love:

   _____

   _____

   _____

2. *What* are you trying to tell the person? (What do you want or need? How can you state what you want using an "I" statement?) _____

   _____

   _____

   _____

3. What can you say to this person so he or she will not misunderstand you or become defensive? What exactly is bothering you? Be specific. (What is your *message?*)

   _____

   _____

   _____

4. Get *feedback* from the person. (Can the person provide you with what you want or need? How does the other person see the problem? What does the other person want or need?) _____

   _____

   _____

   _____

Knowing what your needs are, and sharing those needs with others in your life, will help you have rewarding relationships. Hopefully, communicating with others will go smoothly for you. If these new skills do not work for you, counselors are available who can provide coaching on how to begin solving relationship problems.

■ Section G: Treatments for relationship difficulties

Family and friends can be sources of support, but they can also be sources of stress if problems are not worked out. If you continue to have difficulty being with or talking with your loved ones, help is available. Treatments for relationship difficulties are available that can help you during this time of adjustment. Family and couples therapy can help veterans work out their problems with their loved ones in constructive ways. It helps to have a professional who can be objective and who does not take sides. Family and couples therapy helps give people different ways of looking at things and helps them adjust during difficult times.

▶ When to talk to your doctor

Have you or someone you know been:

- Yelling at your spouse, partner, or other family members a lot lately? Having conflicts that you cannot resolve?
- Feeling disconnected from others, or like no one can understand what you're going through?
- Feeling overwhelmed by your reactions?
- Thinking you might hurt yourself or someone else?

Did you answer YES to ONE or more of these questions? If so, talk to your doctor right away.

▶ The heart of the matter

Many veterans feel very different when they return from a deployment. In fact, many things have changed, both for the veterans and for their families. It takes time to feel comfortable with other people again, and it may also take a while to figure out how to function as a family again. It is important to take time to address specific problems that may be occurring during reintegration with family and friends, including practicing good communication with people who are important to you. Remember to be patient both with yourself and with others.

- Please turn to the end of the chapter and take the quiz. Remember that the quizzes are a good way to review some of the important points in the chapter.

▶ On your own

1. Complete the Phone Calling Exercise. Remember to note your SUDS before and after the calls. Complete details about this exercise are included in the "On Your Own" section at the end of Chapter 1.
2. Your Communication Plan Exercise is your master plan for dealing with conflicts. If you are ready, go ahead and bring up any problem(s) you identified with your family members or friends. You can copy this exercise, or answer these questions in your head when you run into problems with anyone. Use this exercise to help you in having a conversation with someone this week.

Phone Calling Exercise Worksheet

Name: _____

Session Number: _____

Question: _____

Person Called	Date	Your Own SUDS Before (0–10)	Answer/Topic	Call Length	Your Own SUDS After (0–10)

► **Chapter 7—Reintegrating with family and friends quiz**

Name: _____

Date: _____ _____ / _____ _____ / _____ _____

1. Veterans should be able to adjust back to family life easily and immediately after returning from the war zone.
   True or False

2. Which of the following statements is an example of fighting fair?
   a. I feel angry when you tell me not to watch TV because I need time to relax.
   b. You always nag me when I watch TV.
   c. You wouldn't bother me if you loved me.
   d. I feel like you are always nagging me.

3. Which of the following is a common change veterans may experience that may make it more difficult to reintegrate with the family?
   a. Loss of interest in activities that used to be enjoyable
   b. Difficulty trusting and feeling close to others
   c. Feeling a need to be in control at all times
   d. Not showing emotions besides anger
   e. Reluctant to talk about what happened in the war zone
   f. All of the above

4. Name 3 particular problems that frequently make reuniting as a couple, or with children, more difficult after deployment:

   _____

   _____

   _____

5. Name 4 things that may help with the transition back to being with family and friends (for example, making individual time to spend with each child or important family member):

   _____

   _____

   _____

Staying Strong

As human beings, we all have within us an extraordinary ability to grow from our challenges and hard times. In this chapter, we will explore how hardship can help us grow and discover great possibilities in our lives.

▶ Building strength

The experience of combat deployment can be a difficult and painful one. It is common for people going through hardships to want to hurry up and get back to the way things were before. Yet there are also times when people have feelings of doubt that things could ever be the same again.

After being in a war zone, many veterans may wonder if they will ever feel normal again. Veterans may have injuries and losses of physical capabilities; losses of comrades and friends; losses of time with children and separation from loved ones; losses of their job, occupation, or career; or losses of a spouse through divorce. Other losses that veterans may experience in war include losses of innocence or losses of spiritual connectedness. The journey through the pain and grief resulting from such losses can be very difficult.

■ Section A: The meaning of hardships and challenges

When life is difficult, most of us ask one question—"why?" This question has been raised since the beginning of time. When we lose people who mean a lot to us, when we see others suffer, or when we experience our own loss, we need to know the reason for events that cause suffering and pain.

Indeed, most spiritual systems have tried to pinpoint the meaning of suffering and pain. There are many philosophies and religions that address this issue. An important point taken from all of these philosophies and religions is this:

■ Suffering and pain have the potential for creating greater possibilities and helping an individual to grow, should he or she choose to.

Identifying growth can be difficult for veterans who may be feeling depressed and worthless. Letting go of guilt and pain may feel like a betrayal to those who were lost. Veterans who are suffering from depression may have particular difficulty focusing on the positive. If you are still grieving and feel unable to complete this chapter, you should get additional help for depression and grief from a professional, and you may need to wait a little while before finishing this chapter. On the other hand, it is important to remember that it is human nature to avoid difficult topics. As you remember from Chapter 1, avoiding these topics will only maintain your stress symptoms. We encourage you to directly address these topics.

Meaning making

Getting through hardships such as difficult war deployments is admirable, but what happens afterward? What do you do with those experiences now? Work hard at trying to forget everything? Live your life filled with bitterness and anger? Or do you become more understanding of life? Do you become wiser? How do you make meaning out of the experiences you have seen and lived through? Is it possible to transform and actually grow from surviving the hardships of your war experience?

If we look at others who have survived very difficult experiences, we find that most say that many good things have actually happened as a result of their dealing with hardships. This applies to war veterans as well as those who have suffered from other types of severe loss.

■ Section B: Identifying strengths

In addition to problems of combat stress, warriors also return with skills, knowledge, confidence, and a sense of accomplishment that only comes from surviving great hardship and overcoming challenges. Veterans have gained strength, worldliness, confidence, and sometimes even an appreciation for life that they never had before.

Take a look at and answer the following questions about your war experience:

■ What types of lessons or new skills did you learn while you were at war? What types of positive things did you accomplish?

_____

_____

_____

■ What do you see as being your strengths?

_____

_____

_____

■ How do you see yourself using those strengths in the near future?

_____

_____

_____

■ Section C: Identifying values

Our values are the qualities in life that are most important to us. Even though we all have values that guide the way we live our lives, we rarely take a moment to think about what our values are. Values can refer to what is most important in our lives, such as an appreciation of:

■ Your freedom,

■ Your country,

■ Your friends,

■ Your family, and

■ Your God.

As one example, many prisoners of war (POWs) from World War II faced long periods of severe stress, lost friends, and lost years with their families (who may have even assumed they were dead). However, despite the pain and the obvious losses experienced by these heroes, most survivors also said that they grew in some way from being a POW. Values that former POWs gained from their experiences of being in war included:

1. Greater appreciation for freedom,

2. Greater appreciation for family and friends,

3. Greater patience and understanding,

4. More optimism about life, and

5. The ability to know what is important in life, versus what is trivial

Other amazing individuals note positive aspects to similar extraordinarily difficult circumstances. Senator John McCain, during his service in the U.S. Navy received numerous honors—including a Bronze Star, Silver Star, the Legion of Merit, Purple Heart, and the Distinguished Flying Cross. Despite enduring incredible hardship including frequent torture during five and a half years as a P.O.W. during the Vietnam War, he has spoken positively in interviews about his experiences, saying, "I was privileged to observe a thousand acts of courage and compassion and love." He also demonstrates a strong commitment to these values: "To sacrifice for a cause greater than yourself, and to sacrifice your life to the eminence of that cause, is the noblest activity of all."

Everett Alvarez Jr. was the first naval aviator shot down over Vietnam during the Vietnam War, and was held as a POW for eight and half years, enduring hardship and torture until his release in 1973. Mr. Alvarez received numerous awards during his military career, including the Silver Star, two Bronze Stars, two Legions of Merit, two Purple Hearts, and the Distinguished Flying Cross. During an interview for the *Pittsburgh Post Gazette* in 2001 (Urichio, 2001), he was asked how his time as a POW changed him. He responded:

> It was a maturing process. In order to survive the harshness, the terrible things we had to go through, we had to hold onto our core values and beliefs. In doing so, it was a tempering process of our characters. When you come out, you recognize there are obstacles in life, but you work your way through them and press on. You recognize also what's most important in life, and that's having your family and those you love around you. Material wealth is not as important, certainly not as important as health. You recognize how short life is, and how little time you have to go out and do something not only for yourself but for others.

He was also asked if he was angry about having lost over eight years of his life, and said:

> You know, one of the things you learn is that life is full of unexpected occurrences. I could be very angry, but what good would that do? I've always taken the attitude that you look forward and thank God you have your life because a lot of people don't. I have the opportunity to go on and continue my life. It would not behoove me to look back.

Mr. Alvarez has served as the deputy director of the Peace Corps and deputy administrator of the Veterans Administration, as well as founding his own management consulting firm, and co-authoring two books. In his book, *Chained Eagle*—an account of his experiences in Vietnam—Alvarez (2005) writes, "My strength came from holding fast to my faith in God and belief in the values enshrined in our Constitution: duty, loyalty, unity, integrity, honor, allegiance, courage, and hope" (p. 2).

Often situations that produce severe hardship can also produce positive changes and opportunities for growth. This growth can take many forms, including an increase in commitment to positive values.

Values also include principles we live our lives by, such as:

- Being honest
- Doing a good job
- Being a reliable son or daughter
- Being a model citizen
- Being a good parent or spouse or partner
- Respecting elders
- Being a loyal friend

Take some time to think about and answer the following questions:

- What are some important things you have learned from surviving your deployment?

_____

_____

_____

- What kinds of things do you value more now that you have come back from the war?

_____

_____

_____

- List three of the most important values in your life:

_____

_____

_____

We rarely take the time to think about our values. However, the closer we follow our values in our day-to-day lives, the more meaningful our lives can be. For example, one Iraq War veteran said that seeing so much suffering while deployed—and being apart from his family—made him value being a good parent to his young daughter. When he returned home, he recognized that he had lost important friends while in Iraq, and he also recognized the importance of developing close relationships with other friends and loves ones. And because he valued being a good parent, he did his best to:

- Spend time with his daughter
- Speak to his daughter in a respectful way
- Attend school meetings
- Help teach his daughter positive life lessons

For each of the values you listed above, write down exactly how a person who has that value might behave. What would such a person do?

Value	How would a person who has this value behave?
Value No. 1	1.
	2.
	3.
	4.
Value No. 2	1.
	2.
	3.
	4.
Value No. 3	1.
	2.
	3.
	4.

■ Section D: Identifying goals

Your goals are the aims or objectives you have for yourself. However, rarely do we sit back and think about what goals we have for our lives and which goals might be best for us. Goals that are best for us will be consistent with our values and will help us meet our needs in some way. What do you want to achieve with your life?

Before you went to war, you may have had goals for what you wanted to accomplish in life. Goals might have included:

- Getting a good job
- Learning a trade
- Getting a college degree

- Getting married
- Having children

- What goals did you have for yourself *before* you went to war?

  _____

  _____

  _____

- Have these goals changed?

  _____

  _____

  _____

- List three goals that you have for your life now?

  _____

  _____

  _____

There are many goals in life that we dream about. For example, when you were young you might have had a goal to become a millionaire. As adults, it is important for us to choose goals that really make sense and that are achievable. Additionally, you must choose a goal that you are willing to work toward. When you have a short-term goal, you must be willing to complete the work that it takes to reach it. For example, imagine that a veteran named Bill wants to complete four college courses. He must show up for class, pay attention in class, complete homework, and study for exams.

When we have a long-term goal, we choose behaviors that help us reach those goals. For example, if Bill wants to get a college degree, he must first take the courses he needs to qualify for college. He must obtain the finances to pay for college. And he must complete all the courses that are required for his degree.

For at least one of the goals you listed above, write down exactly what steps need to be taken to reach that goal.

Goal	What steps should a person who has this goal take?
Goal No. 1	1.
	2.
	3.
	4.
Goal No. 2	1.
	2.
	3.
	4.
Goal No. 3	1.
	2.
	3.
	4.

If you are grieving or suffering from depression, it may be difficult for you to set goals. Do your best. Again, those who are still grieving and feel unable to complete this chapter should see a professional who can provide help for their depression and grief, and may need to wait a little while before finishing this chapter.

▶ When to talk to your doctor

Have you or someone you know been:

- Feeling trapped, suffocated, closed-in, or panicky when you are in closed-in areas or crowds?
- Feeling angry at or disconnected from others, or like no one can understand what you're going through?
- Feeling overwhelmed by your reactions?
- Thinking you might hurt yourself or someone else?

Did you answer YES to ONE or more of these questions? If so, talk to your doctor right away.

▶ The heart of the matter

Your war deployment(s) will likely be among the most significant experiences of your life. Many veterans from other eras often feel that their combat experience played a critical role in their developing into a mature adult with positive character and strong values. Often they describe their war experiences as including some of the *best* experiences of their lives—even if going to war also included the *worst* experiences of their lives.

Your view of the world is now different. Your view of yourself and others will now be different. It will take time to see the broader significance your role made to your country. Over time you will gain the perspective to understand how immensely profound this experience really has been, and how much strength you truly possess.

■ Please turn to the end of the chapter and take the quiz.

▶ On your own

It is now time to put together all the skills you learned from this book. Continue to use the skills you learned in your everyday life. Remember to set positive goals for different ways that you can challenge yourself each day—daily practice, daily training, and daily healing.

▶ **Chapter 8—Staying strong quiz**

Name: _____

Date: _____ _____ / _____ _____ / _____ _____

1. List four positive things that you learned about yourself when you were deployed?
   (e.g., courage, ability to protect yourself, discipline).

   1. _____
   2. _____
   3. _____
   4. _____

2. What do you want your life to look like five years from now? Name four goals you
   have for yourself.

   1. _____
   2. _____
   3. _____
   4. _____

3. In this chapter, you identified some of your values, and ways a person who has
   those values might behave. What are some things you can do in the weeks and
   months ahead, or ways you can behave, that are consistent with your values?

   1. _____
   2. _____
   3. _____
   4. _____

Veteran Resource Guide

▶ Veteran Affairs (VA) resources

■ VA medical centers

The VA Medical Center system's specialized PTSD clinics and programs can provide to eligible veterans educational information, diagnostic assessment and treatment for PTSD and other mental health and medical disorders. Following deployment to a combat zone after discharge, if a returnee has enrolled for VA services, he or she should be qualified for two years of care for conditions potentially related to your service. Both VA medical centers and Vet Centers provide veterans with mental-health services that health insurance will cover or that costs little or nothing, according to a veteran's ability to pay. To find a VA Medical Center near you, call 1-800-905-4675 or look on the web at www1.va.gov/directory/guide/home.asp?isFlash=1.

■ Vet centers

Community-based Vet Centers provide benefits information, evaluations, and treatment for trauma to any veteran who served in a war zone or in a military conflict (such as in Panama, Grenada, or Somalia). There are no co-payments or charges of any kind for Vet Center confidential services. Vet Centers also provide trauma counseling for veterans who were sexually harassed or sexually assaulted while on active duty. To find a Vet Center near you, call 1-800-905-4675 or look on the web also at www1.va.gov/directory/guide/home.asp?isFlash=1.

■ Tragedy Assistance Program for Survivors (TAPS)

The Tragedy Assistance Program for Survivors (TAPS) is a nonprofit Veterans Service Organization that provides a wide range of free services to all those affected by the death of a loved one in the armed forces. To find a TAPS program call 1-800-959-TAPS (1-800-959-8277) or look on the web at www.TAPS.org.

■ Office of Veterans services

The Office of Veterans Services Acts as a liaison between the Department of Veterans Affairs and individual veterans and between the governor and veterans' organizations. Assist veterans in obtaining State and federal entitlements, supply the latest information on veterans' issues and provide advice and support to veterans making the transition back into civilian life.

■ **VA benefits**

To find out more about VA health benefits, call 1-877-222-VETS. The web provides information about VA Medical Center in your area at www.va.gov/rcs/. The VA also offers the MyHealtheVet and Seamless Transition web sites, full of helpful online information for veterans and family members.

▶ **Military resources**

Clients who are Active Duty can access their installation's support services for information about where to find mental health services. Larger installations will have a military treatment facility on-site that may provide treatment for PTSD. Many of these centers provide individual, group, marriage, and family counseling. These might include:

- Air Force Life Skills Clinics
- Army Community Centers
- Marine Corps Community Services
- U.S. Coast Guard Work-Life Center

Additionally, family programs may be available to support to families in military and civilian settings. Such centers also can provide information and updates on available benefits, entitlements, and services (medical care, etc.). These might include:

- Airman and Family Readiness Programs
- Army Family Advocacy Programs
- Army National Guard
- State Family Program Office
- Fleet and Family Support Center
- Marine & Family Services Counseling Services

■ **Military ONESOURCE**

An organization that provides services including brief counseling to active duty military personnel, including Reservists and the National Guard (1-800-342-9647; www.military-onesource.com).

▶ **Community resources**

Important questions to ask a potential therapist include:

- What experience do you have working with war returnees with trauma and or PTSD?
- Do you have any specialized training in PTSD treatment?
- What kinds of PTSD treatments do you use?

Here are some websites that can help to locate a qualified therapist in your area:

- **The Association for Advancement of Behavioral and Cognitive Therapies** (ABCT, formerly AABT) is a professional organization that maintains a referral source for therapists with advanced training in Cognitive Behavioral Therapy. You can also list the area you need special help with, such as PTSD, to locate a therapist with special expertise. They are located on the web at www.abct.org.

- **Sidran** is a nonprofit trauma organization that offers a referral list of professional therapists, as well as a fact sheet on how to choose a therapist for PTSD and dissociative disorders at www.sidran.org.

- **The American Psychological Association** also offers a list of referrals by area at http://locator.apa.org/terms.cfm.

- *Psychology Today* lists therapists at http://therapists.psychologytoday.com/ppc/prof_search.php?iorb=4764/.

- **Community Mental Health Centers** may be available in your area. You can find a center near you at the Center for Mental Health Services Locator site at www.mentalhealth.samhsa.gov/databases/.

Finally, another way to locate a therapist is to make phone calls in your area to:

- Your local mental-health agency or family physician.
- Your local state psychological association.
- A local university or college department of psychology.
- If you are a member of a Health Maintenance Organization (HMO), call to find out if mental-health services are available.

▶ Web resources

The National Center for Post-Traumatic Stress Disorder is a comprehensive source for information related to PTSD developed by leaders in the field of PTSD. The website contains over 200 pages, 125 fact sheets, 400 downloadable articles, videos, and a searchable database of 25,000+ articles at National Center for Post-Traumatic Stress Disorder: www.ncptsd.va.org.

The Iraqi War Clinician's Guide in a treatment guide developed collaboratively by top clinicians and researchers in the Department of Defense and the National Center for PTSD. The guide contains numerous articles on the assessment and treatment of OIF/OEF returnees. It is an excellent resource for clinicians who are addressing various issues posed by returnees. You can find it on the NC-PTSD website at www.ncptsd.va.org.

Battlemind.org training helps recent returning veterans to develop a realistic preview, in the form of a briefing, of the stresses and strains of deployment on Soldiers. It is developed by leading military professionals at Walter Reed Army Institute of Research. Four training briefs are available for soldiers, leaders, National Guard/Reserves, and families at www.battlemind.org.

Courage to Care is an electronic health campaign for military and civilian professionals serving the military community, as well as for military men, women and families. Courage to Care at www.usuhs.mil/psy/courage.html consists of electronic fact sheets on health topics relevant to military life. Courage to Care content is developed by leading military health experts from Uniformed Services University of the Health Sciences, your nation's federal medical school.

Another good online resource is *webmd.com*. Veterans can go into this site and search for stress management techniques. It has hundreds of additional resources at www.webmd.com.

Chapter Quizzes Answer Key

▶ **Chapter 1—Understanding Transition Stress Reactions Quiz**

Answer Key

1. What term refers to going out of our way *not* to think about or to keep away from something:

   a. Hypervigilance

   b. **Avoidance**

   c. Reexperiencing

   d. Dropping out

2. It's very unusual to experience unwanted memories after returning from the war zone.

   ■ **False:** Following combat or other highly stressful experiences, several types of reexperiencing symptoms are quite common—including intrusive thoughts, memories, dreams, and nightmares.

3. Although reminders of stressful combat events can feel overwhelming, the reaction to reminders often lessens with time.

   ■ **True:** Common initial reactions to highly stressful events, including combat, can feel quite overwhelming. However, in most cases, they lessen over time. If they persist, or are severe, it may be important to seek additional treatment.

4. Isolating from other people means loss of support, friendship, and closeness with others, and more time to worry or feel hopeless and alone.

   ■ **True:** Although the desire to isolate and avoid is a common reaction to combat stress, isolation can be very harmful in terms of reducing support and increasing opportunities for rumination and feelings of worry and loneliness.

5. What does SUDS stand for?

   a. Strong Underpinnings of Denial and Suppression

   b. **Subjective Units of Distress Scale**

c. The stuff you find floating at the top of beer

d. Soap scum Under Da Sink

6. Working all the time to try to avoid distressing memories of the stressful event is a good way to deal with post-war stress.

- **False:** As with other forms of avoidance, working all of the time typically serves to prolong the effects of transition stress. Thus, although staying active can be a helpful part of successful coping, using work (or anything else) as a means to avoid addressing transition stress results in fewer opportunities for positive experiences and feelings of achievement.

▶ Chapter 2—Stress Management Quiz

Answer Key

1. What are some common symptoms of long-term stress?

   a. Irritability

   b. Upset stomach, nausea, diarrhea

   c. Stiff neck or headaches

   d. **All of these are common**

2. Which of these are **positive ways** to cope with stress?

   a. **Exercise**

   b. Driving fast in your car

   c. Drinking a case of beer

   d. All of these are a positive way to cope with stress

3. Which of these are **negative ways** to cope with stress?

   a. Obsessing or worrying about things

   b. Smoking marijuana

   c. Road raging

   d. **All of these are not good**

4. What would be an example of a **mind-centered** stress management skill?

   a. Guided imagery

   b. Self-hypnosis

   c. Autogenics

   d. **All of these are mind-centered skills**

5. This is a relaxation skill where you breathe in with your belly coming out, and exhaling and your belly coming back in. It is very easy and helps people to relax. **What is it called?**

   a. Autoreflex breathing

   b. Deep muscle breathing

   c. **Diaphragmatic breathing**

   d. Exhalation Therapy

Answer Key

1. Reactive coping tools are behaviors that we use to prepare ourselves for problems that might occur in the future.

   ■ **False:** This is a description of proactive coping tools. Reactive coping tools are skills and behaviors that we do in response to a problem.

2. Social isolation helps protect a person from problems, and is a good way to help a person adjust to being back home after a deployment.

   ■ **False:** A person's mood and overall adjustment to being back from a deployment will be improved by social activities and resisting the urge to isolate. Social activities are healthy for the brain, and also provide more opportunities for positive experiences with others.

3. Setting and achieving goals is an important way to improve mood and decrease depression.

   ■ **True:** Even meeting small and moderate goals can help to produce a feeling of empowerment and mastery that helps to break the spiral of depression and start making positive changes.

4. When a person feels anxious in a situation that used to be comfortable, it means that they should get out of that situation as quickly as they can, and avoid that situation in the future.

   ■ **False:** Remember that after highly stressful events, the part of the brain called the amygdala sometimes becomes overactive and produces feelings of anxiety and fear even when nothing is going wrong. As a result, people may avoid doing things that were related to danger in a warzone, but that will not really lead to danger back home—such as being in crowds, going to movie theaters, or sitting with ones back to the door. However, it is important to help our brain and body learn the difference between what is dangerous and what is merely uncomfortable. The only way to do this is to practice being active again and give ourselves the chance to relearn that most activities are safe. This means *not* avoiding situations that may cause anxiety, but which are not actually dangerous.

5. As soon as we start doing pleasant activities, we should expect that our mood will change completely, and everything will be okay.

   ■ **False:** the positive spiral of activities that help reduce depression and elevate overall mood can be a slow process. It is important to remember that at first activities may not feel very good—this is part of feeling depressed. However, over time, with positive actions our mood improves, motivation increases, and even the activities themselves become more pleasurable.

6. When we experience very few activities we consider to be pleasant, we are more likely feel depressed. Also, when we feel depressed, we do not feel like doing the kinds of activities that are likely to be a source of pleasure. This is known as the:

   a. Complicated bereavement

   b. Sliding depressive cycle

c. **Downward spiral of depression**

d. Resilient coping

▶ Chapter 4—Sleep Quiz

Answer Key

1. We have dreams every night that we sleep.
   - **True:** Although most people do not remember their dreams, we all dream in cycles throughout the night

2. Sleeping in late is a good way to catch up on lost sleep.
   - **False:** Sleeping in late will interfere with the sleep cycle.

3. Alcohol and certain medications (such as Valium, Xanax, and over-the-counter sleep medications) can mess up our sleep cycle.
   - **True:** Although alcohol and certain sleep medications put us out, they work against our natural sleep cycle so that we do not feel restored after sleeping.

4. Antidepressants can mess up our sleep cycle.
   - **False:** Antidepressants (e.g., Wellbutrin, Lexapro, Prozac, Paxil) actually help restore our natural sleep cycle.

5. Taking a 60-minute nap can mess up the sleep cycle.
   - **True:** Taking naps longer than 30 minutes tends to interfere with the sleep cycle in the evening.

6. If you cannot fall asleep at night, it is best to perform a stressful, highly demanding task that will tire you out and help you fall asleep.
   - **False:** High demanding and stressful tasks will increase hormones like cortisol, which increase alertness and make it harder to fall asleep.

7. If you wake up and cannot get back to sleep, it is best to get out of bed (even in the middle of the night) and engage in a light, somewhat boring, activity.
   - **True:** It is best to perform a boring, nonstressful activity, such as reading a light novel, to prepare the body for sleep. Likewise, if you wake up at night and cannot get back to sleep, it is best to get out of bed (even in the middle of the night) and perform some nonstressful activity until you feel sleepy.

8. One way to cope with a nightmare is to write it down.
   - **True:** Writing down a nightmare makes the dream less real and helps you calm down faster. It can also be helpful to share the dream with someone close to you.

▶ Chapter 5—Dealing with Anger Quiz

Answer Key

1. Being angry for long period of time may lead to:
   a. High blood pressure
   b. Early death

    c. Stomach disorders

    d. **All of the above**

2. Which of the following is an **unhelpful** thing to do when you get very angry?

    a. Count to 10

    b. Take a time out

    c. **Try to argue your point**

    d. All of the above

3. Which of the following is a **helpful** use of your anger?

    a. Use anger to help you work harder

    b. Use anger to help motivate you to reach a goal

    c. Use anger to help you solve a problem

    d. **All of the above**

4. If your anger level is 5 or over (on a scale from 1 to 10) you should perform a healthy coping behavior.

    - **True:** When our anger goes above a 5, our thinking and our overall level of functioning is actually lowered. In addition to damage to our body from chronic anger, we are also more likely to act in foolish ways and get into more trouble. Using coping skills to reduce our anger when it begins to escalate helps us to manage situations better.

5. Returnees coming home from the war zone tend to be very calm and relaxed.

    - **False:** People returning from deployments often feel angry, on edge, and hyperalert. These are expected reactions that many people have following chronic stress in a combat zone, where anger may have often provided energy needed to survive life-threatening situations.

6. Anger is a "bad" emotion that can only lead to conflict and aggression.

    - **False:** Anger that is expressed in helpful ways can be very healthy. Channeled in a healthy way, anger can be used to give people energy, to help them reach their goals, and can motivate people to work harder, or help people to handle emergencies.

7. Name 3 cues that tell people when they are becoming angry:

    - **Responses will vary, and may include a broad range of physiological and cognitive cues.**

▶ **Chapter 6—Reintegrating with Society Quiz**

Answer Key

1. People who are hypervigilant:

    a. Always help other people who are in need

    b. Think they are sick even when they are well.

c. **Are overly alert for danger even when danger is not present.**

d. All of the above.

2. We can control every aspect of our environment and our life.

- **False:** There are many factors in life that are beyond our control. For example, one may not have control over where one is stationed, when and for how long one is deployed, other people's behavior in general, crowds, the weather, etc. After a deployment, other things may have changed as well, including the possibility of such things as not being in control of when memories of stressful events occur.

3. "Thinking" ahead is an important part of making healthy decisions and reintegrating with society.

- **True:** There are several predictable problems that may occur—for example, difficulties with friends and family, antimilitary statements or other offensive and insensitive statements, etc. Anticipating these types of problems and problem solving in advance how one might handle these situations, can help to head off numerous problems before they begin.

4. What are some situations or people that trigger stress reactions for you?

- Responses will vary.

5. What healthy coping behaviors can I use to deal with the people and/or situations that trigger stress reactions?
Examples include:

- Communication skills

- Time-outs

- Other coping behaviors from earlier chapters

▶ Chapter 7—Reintegrating with Family and Friends Quiz

Answer Key

1. Veterans should be able to adjust back to family life easily and immediately after returning from the war zone.

- **False:** Given that both veterans and their families undergo changes during a deployment, it is natural for both to take time to readjust to being back together again.

2. Which of the following statements is an example of fighting fair?

a. **I feel angry when you tell me not to watch TV because I need time to relax.**

b. You always nag me when I watch TV.

c. You would not bother me if you loved me.

d. I feel like you are always nagging me.

3. Which of the following is a common change veterans may experience that may make it more difficult to reintegrate with the family:

    a. Loss of interest in activities that used to be enjoyable

    b. Difficulty trusting and feeling close to others

    c. Feeling a need to be in control at all times

    d. Not showing emotions besides anger

    e. Reluctant to talk about what happened in the war zone

    f. **All of the above**

4. Name 3 particular problems that frequently make reuniting as a couple, or with children, more difficult after deployment.

    Examples include:

    - Face to face communication may be hard at first.

    - Sexual closeness may also be awkward at first.

    - Losing interest in sexual activities, which may lead to your spouse or partner feeling hurt.

    - You may feel closer to your friends, and feel like your spouse or partner is a stranger.

    - Roles for basic household chores may have changed.

    - Spouses or partners may have become more independent and learned new coping skills.

    - You may have changed in your outlook and priorities in life.

    - Children have grown and may be different in many ways.

    - Your children may not recognize you, or may be slow to hug you.

    - Children may be very clingy, act younger than they are, or act indifferent, as if they do not care.

5. Name 4 things that may help with the transition back to being with family and friends (for example, making individual time to spend with each child or important family member).

    Examples include:

    - Taking time to listen to your spouse or partner, children, and other important family members.

    - Making individual time for each child and other important family members.

    - Taking time, such as a whole day away, for just you and your spouse or partner to renew your relationship.

    - Going slowly when reestablishing your place in the family.

    - Making efforts to explain to your family what you are feeling and what you would like.

    - Sharing with your family some stories about your deployment.

    - Supporting good things your family has done while you were gone.

    - Being prepared to make some adjustments.

► **Chapter 8—Staying Strong Quiz**

Answer Key

1. Name four positive things that you learned about yourself when you were deployed? (e.g., courage, ability to protect yourself, discipline).

   ■ Responses will vary.

2. What do you want your life to look like five years from now? Name four goals you have for yourself.

   ■ Responses will vary.

3. In this chapter, you identified some of your values, and ways **a** person who has those values might behave. Name some things you can do in the weeks and months ahead that are consistent with your values?

   ■ Responses will vary.

Stress Management Handouts

▶ **Identifying Stress Cues Worksheet**

A very important part of monitoring our stress is to identify how we react to things that happen in our lives. These are what we call "cues" because, if we pay attention to them, we will be able to know that we are in a high-stress situation. Please fill out each cue so that you can become more aware of what sets you off and stresses you out.

1. Physical cues (how your body responds to stress; e.g., increased heart rate, tightness in chest, upset stomach, feeling hot)

   _____

   _____

   _____

2. Behavioral cues (what your body does; e.g., raised voice, clenched teeth/fist, pacing)

   _____

   _____

   _____

3. Emotional cues (feelings that come up; e.g., fear, anger, sadness, guilt)

   _____

   _____

   _____

4. Cognitive (thinking) cues (what we think about in response to the event; e.g., negative self-talk such as "I'm going to lose control," "I've got to get out of here," "I can't handle this")

   _____

   _____

   _____

   _____

▶ Identifying Stressful Events Worksheet

To manage your stress well, it is really important that you pay attention to and identify situations that make you feel anxious, nervous, or angry. Most of us are aware that there are certain "hot situations" we avoid because they make us feel uncomfortable.

The purpose of this worksheet is to help you define those "hot situations" *for you,* and how to identify when your anxiety or anger is being provoked. Sometimes these situations remind us of things that have happened in the past where we felt particularly anxious or angry.

1. What events or situations in the past have triggered a stress reaction in you?

   _____

   _____

   _____

2. What "hot situations" currently trigger a stress reaction in you?

   _____

   _____

   _____

▶ Weekly Stress Monitoring Worksheet

Use this sheet to record your stress during the week. You can still use this sheet in session to discuss what occurred that caused your stress to rise and what you did to manage the stress reaction. This can also be used to help you develop additional strategies to deal with similar situations in the future.

1. What was the highest number you reached on the Stress Meter during the past week?

   _____

   _____

   _____

2. What was the event that triggered your stress?

   _____

   _____

   _____

3. What cues were associated with the stress-inducing event?

    a. Physical Cues

    b. Behavioral Cues

    c. Emotional Cues

    d. Cognitive Cues

4. What strategies did you use to prevent hitting a 10 on the Stress Meter (assuming you did not hit a 10)?

_____

_____

_____

5. For each day this week, monitor and record the highest number you reach on the Stress Meter.

_____ Monday

_____ Tuesday

_____ Wednesday

_____ Thursday

_____ Friday

_____ Saturday

_____ Sunday

▶ Monitoring Stress and SUDS

Monitoring stress level is much like checking a temperature gauge on the wall inside your home. In order to effectively cope with your stress it is important to be aware of how stressed you are feeling. The gauge that we use to monitor stress or distress level is the subjective units of distress (SUDS).

What is your SUDS level right now, on a scale of 1 to 10—with 1 being very low stress and 10 being that you are so uncomfortable that you can hardly stand it?

Please refer to the SUDS scale below at this time. This will be the way that stress or distress level will be monitored or checked from time to time.

Completely Calm   Nervous Wreck

0   1   2   3   4   5   6   7   8   9   10

References

Alvarez, E., & Pitch, A. S. (2005). *Chained eagle: The heroic story of the first American shot down over North Vietnam.* Washington, DC: Potomac Books.

Beck, A. T. (1988). *Love is never enough.* New York: Harper & Row.

Beck, J. S. (1995). *Cognitive therapy: Basics and beyond.* New York: Guilford Press.

Davis, J. L., & Wright, D. C. (2007). Randomized clinical trial for treatment of chronic nightmares in trauma-exposed adults. *Journal of Traumatic Stress, 20*(2), 123–133.

Edleson, J. L., & Tolman, R. M. (1992). *Interventions for men who batter: An ecological approach.* Newbury Park, CA: Sage.

Gottman, J. M., & Silver, N. (1999). *The seven principles for making marriage work.* New York: Three Rivers Press.

Gray, J. A. (1988). *The psychology of fear and stress* (2nd ed.). Cambridge: Cambridge University Press.

Guerney, B. (1977). *Relationship enhancement.* San Francisco: Jossey-Bass.

Jacobs, G. D. (1998). *Say good night to insomnia.* New York: Henry Holt.

Jacobson, N. S., & Christensen, A. (1996). *Acceptance and change in couple therapy: A therapist's guide to transforming relationships.* New York: Norton.

Krystal, A. D., & Davidson, J. R. T. (2007). The use of Prazosin for the treatment of trauma nightmares and sleep disturbance in combat veterans with post-traumatic stress disorder. *Biological Psychiatry, 61*(8), 925–927.

LeDoux, J. (2002). *Synaptic self: How our brains become who we are.* New York: Penguin Books.

Lewinsohn, P. M., Hoberman, H., Teri, L., & Hautziner, M. (1985). An integrative theory of depression. In S. Reiss & R. Bootzine (Eds.), *Theoretical issues in behavior therapy* (p. 176). New York: Academic Press.

Library of Congress. (2007, May 29). Video interview with John S. McCain, III. In *Stories from the Veterans History Project.* Retrieved September 24, 2007, from http://lcweb2.loc.gov/diglib/vhp-stories/loc.natlib.afc2001001.07736/.

Paymar, M. (1993). *Violent no more: Helping men end domestic abuse.* Alameda, CA: Hunter House.

Pence, E., & Paymar, M. (1993). *Education groups for men who batter: The Duluth Model.* New York: Springer.

Resick, P. A., & Schnicke, M. K. (1993). *Cognitive processing therapy for rape victims: A treatment manual.* Newbury Park, CA: Sage.

Rosenbaum, A., & Leisring, P. A. (2001). Group intervention programs for batterers. In R. A. Geffner & A. Rosenbaum (Eds.), *Domestic violence offenders: Current interventions, research, and implications for policies and standards* (pp. 57–72). New York: Haworth Press.

Rothbaum, B. O., Foa, E. B., Riggs, D. S., Murdock, T., & Walsh, W. (1992). A prospective examination of posttraumatic stress disorder in rape victims. *Journal of Traumatic Stress, 5,* 455–475.

Seligman, M. E. (1991). Power and powerlessness: Comments on "cognates of personal control." *Applied and Preventive Psychology, 1,* 119–120.

Uricchio, M. (2001, July 9). Breakfast with . . . Everett Alvarez, Jr. *Pittsburgh Post Gazette.*

Wolpe, J. (1973). *The practice of behavior therapy* (2nd ed.). New York: Pergamon Press.

A Personal Note from the Authors

By surviving war, you survived one of the most profound and challenging experiences anyone can ever face. This, in itself, makes you a strong person.

Our wish for you is that you continue to use the insights gained from this program to your advantage as you face daily challenges. You certainly possess the inner strengths and innate abilities to deal with your life after the war. Focus on your own healing, use the skills you have learned through this program again and again, and know that you can be a person who has the very best in life.

It is our deepest, most sincere hope that you will find healing, peace, and greater inner resilience in your life after war.

Thank you again for your service and commitment to our nation.

Julia M. Whealin, PhD
Lorie T. DeCarvalho, PhD
Edward M. Vega, PhD

Index

Printed in the United States of America
ED-10-27-10